THE WEIGHT OF DEATH
Story Of The Spirit Eyes Series

'Dipo Toby Alakija

© Copyright 2016 by Dipo Toby Alakija.

All rights reserved by Calvary Rock Resources. No part of this book may be reproduced or transmitted in any form or by any means without written permission of the publisher through any of the addresses below, apart from the use of short quotations or occasional page copying for personal or group study.

ISBN: 978-36348-0-1
ISBN: 978-978-36348-0-0

Printed in United States
Published by the publishing house of
CALVARY ROCK RESOURCES

19, Ajina Street, Ikenne Remo,
Ogun State,
Nigeria.

36, Thomson road
Gorton
Manchester
M18 7QQ
United Kingdom

270 Madison Avenue
Suite 1500, New York, NY 10016
United States

www.calvaryrock.org

INTRODUCTION OF THE PLAYS

So many mysterious events are taking place all over the world, which no one can possibly explain unless they are viewed with the spirit eyes. The knowledge of man is limited by what he can see, feel, hear or perceive in other ways. The human senses of perceptions make some people to conclude that God and things of the spirit do not exist. Despite the fact that mankind is troubled by things that are orchestrated in the spirit realm, most people are still oblivious of the forces of darkness and also of the light. While some, especially Christians are very conscious of the spirit realm, a host of others are simply blindfolded by philosophical and scientific explanations. Religion, History, Science, Literature, Arts and Cultures claim to have answers to virtually every phenomenon, including the formation of the of the entire universe, but events like appearances of ghosts and practices of sorceries, witchcraft and occult are getting people more confused. Entertainment industries, especially movie producers make things worse in their claim to relieve the confusion of mankind about the mysterious events. The arrogance in the claim to possess answers to many questions about life as we can perceive them in so many films and the refusal of screen writers to make thorough research on things that bother on mankind before scripting movies make it easy to deceive and mislead billions of people across the globe. To undo the negative impacts of entertainment industries in the human brains all over the world, equal if not more of years of their efforts and financial investments would be required.

The Story Of The Spirit Eyes Series are, therefore, introduced to readers with the main objective of bringing into live scenarios that are mysterious and obscure to most people. It is hoped that the cause of mysterious events such as what makes people go through traumatic experiences would be made open.

These plays, just like most other drama books in this series are inspired either by true life stories or results of my research works into the realm of the spirits. Hence, I want you to consider them as eye openers that bring into light what is happening in the dark and think about the dreamful implications if the messages are ignored or neglected.

I honestly consider it a privilege to share the lessons in these plays with you. Please, enjoy yourself as you get edified.

-Pastor Dipo Toby Alakija
The Playwright

Horror
IN THE FAMILY

BAD CHOICE

Someone made a bad choice
But I am going to pay for it
Someone dined with the devil
But I am going to foot the bill!
What kind of life is this?
What hope do I have?

Someone ate the bad fruit
But I feel the pain in my teeth!
Someone locked me in the house
And set the house on fire!
What kind of life is this?
What hope do I have?

Someone joined the secret cult
And demanded for my head
Someone did the wrong thing
And put our lives on the line!
What kind of life is this?
What hope do I have?

PROLOGUE

NARRATOR: *(stands before the audience as he addresses the people.)* We are in the age of insanity, the time people expect the right thing to happen while they do the wrong thing. Life is like a farm where we reap what we sow. Most parents have sown the wrong things into the lives of their children and they are reaping the dividends. There are so much atrocities that serve as dividends of what parents have sown in the lives of their children. The nucleus family that begins with a couple, extending into chains of families that constitute a community often times begin with the wrong steps. The wrong steps lead to wrong set-ups of families. The wrong set-ups lead to unpleasant environments which invariably take their tolls on the entire nation.

With the case study of a man who took a wrong step by joining a secret cult, the play attempts to educate adults how the bad decision of a father can wipe out the entire family. It also depicts how determination to do the right can bring about survival in the midst of chaos.

Although the play is a very colourfully painted version of a true life story but it has all the elements of truth that can make you survive the ocean of insanity in case you are in this position. The play offers a solution to the mountain-size problems that may be caused by wrong decisions, bad set-up or unpleasant environment.

The play is strictly for adults and youths above fifteen. Sit back and take a journey to and fro the realms of the spirit and the physical. *(He bows, leaving the stage. The audience gives him rounds of applause.)*

SCENE ONE A

(Lando, the head of the brotherhood cult and five other members sit at the secret room that is filled with different occult and fetish items.)

LANDO: *(looks silently round at the rest.)* It is now exactly seven weeks since the brotherhood is reduced to six with the passing away of Talimi, the great warrior. The cause of his death is not quite clear to us despite all we did to find out. That's not the issue right now, however. The issue before us is the membership of the brotherhood that must be up to seven of us. As it is our law, we don't just get someone to replace a member that is gone. It has to be his first son. If he doesn't have a son, it must be the first son of his brother or sister. *(He becomes silent. He stands up, looking thoughtful as if recalling an incidence.)* Talimi told me about his successor in the brotherhood when I asked him...

SCENE TWO (FLASH BACK)

TALIMI: *(stands with Lando beside a jeep outside his house.)* My first child, Damola, as you know is the man that's to replace me in the brotherhood when I'm gone.

LANDO: Why haven't you presented him for initiation into the heir brotherhood?

TALIMI: *(looks regretful.)* I'm trying my best but the young man is stubborn and crazy about his religion.

LANDO: Are you saying he's giving you problem?

TALIMI: Yes… but it's not the type I cannot handle.

LANDO: You sound as if the problem is too big for you to tackle. Do you want us to come in?

TALIMI: Oh, no. Let me exhaust all the means to persuade him, including handing over my business empire to him...

SCENE ONE B

(Lando returns from the flashback and continues.)

LANDO: *(points at the empty chair.)* That chair belongs to Talimi. He has vacated the place for Damola, his son but here we are with no one to fill it. *(He stands up, pacing round and then goes to sit down again.)* I tried to find out why Talimi failed to perform his duty as our member, Danjaruwa told me Damola is a problem - a very big one. Unless we make him occupy his father's seat, the brotherhood will go into... *(He stops abruptly to look at the rest who look*

expectant.) **Extinction!**
THE REST: No!
TALIMI: Calm down, brothers. I didn't say that to harass you or underrate our strength but you have to know we have a very serious threat in our hands. You know I don't point out problems without first thinking of solution. So we're going to send a spirit that will appear as Talimi's ghost. He will trouble the entire family, including his wife until we get Damola to occupy his father's seat. *(He smiles and then spreads his hands.)* What do you say? *(Two of them start clapping. The rest join them one after the other.)*

SCENE THREE
(Bolade lies down on the bed in the room at night, switching off the beside lamp. After a while, there is a gentle breeze blowing the window curtain, making hissing sound. She looks puzzled and puts on the beside lamp again. She stands up and goes to see if the window is opened. It is closed, making her to look more puzzled. As she goes back to the bed, Talimi appears by the window. Bolade screams when she sees him and makes for the door. The door is locked by itself.)

TALIMI: Why are you running away from me?
BOLADE: *(looks frantic.)* You - you are dead.
TALIMI: Dead or not, I am still your husband.
BOLADE: N-no….no!
TALIMI: Listen, I'm here to warn you of the danger that would befall you and our children.
BOLADE: *(calms down a little.)* What danger?
TALIMI: I belong to a group of brotherhood that is behind all the successes we've enjoyed so far. Damola is to succeed me in the group. The group will pay you a visit very soon. If Damola refuses to occupy the position in the group, there would be deaths and horror in the family. *(Talimi disappears. The place becomes calm again, making Bolade to look more confused.)*

SCENE FOUR A
(In the morning, Damola sits at the dinning table with his two brothers, Sesan, Dimeji and two sisters Dolapo and Yinka. They are about to take their meal.)
DAMOLA: *(looks at Yinka.)* Did you inform mother that the food is served?
YINKA: I sent Lara…

DAMOLA: You're supposed to tell her by yourself instead of sending the maid.
SESAN: Does it really matter who delivers the message?
DAMOLA: What did she say?
YINKA: She's still on the bed.
DAMOLA: *(waves indifferently.)* See what I mean. *(He stands up.)* I better check what kept her late on the bed. *(**Bolade comes into the sitting room as he is about to leave. She still looks bewildered.**)* I was just coming to see you. What's wrong, mum? You look as if you've seen a ghost.
BOLADE: *(in a quiet voice.)* Indeed I saw the ghost of your father last night. *(Damola laughs.)* It's true.
DAMOLA: It's okay. Would you come over to the dinning table for breakfast?
BOLADE: *(**goes to join the rest who greet her in diverse ways. She sits down and looks at Damola who also takes his seat.**)* You don't believe me, do you?
DAMOLA: We are getting late for office, mum. So let's pray and eat. We'll talk about it later.
BOLADE: This is important to me, Damola!
SESAN: *(looks at Damola.)* If it's so important to her, let's hear her then.
BOLADE: The spirit of your father appeared to me when I was about to sleep last night. He told me a few things which I must tell you. *(**She is silent for a while and the rest look expectantly at her.**)* He said he belonged to a group before he died. His position in the group needs to be occupied by you. *(**She looks at Damola.**)* According to him, if you refuse to occupy it, there would be horror and death in the family. *(**There is silence.**)* I was told the representatives of the group would soon pay us a visit.
DAMOLA: *(looks round at the rest.)* Shall we pray now?
BOLADE: *(looks impatient.)* Is that all you're going to say?
DAMOLA: I don't know what to say that'll not prolong the matter. We'll talk about it later.
BOLADE: You sound as if you know something about this. *(**There is silence.**)*
SESAN: *(looks at Damola.)* Tell us if you know anything.
DAMOLA: We're supposed to be on our way to the office by now.
DOLAPO: This seems more important than the office commitments. *(Damola looks silently at the food.)*
YINKA: Brother, tell us what you know about this.

DAMOLA: Okay... okay. The group is a secret cult of brotherhood, made up of only seven members. The cult has a small branch that is made up of the heirs of the members in case anyone of them dies. Father tried to make me a member of the small branch but I told him point blank that I'm not only a born-again Christian but one of the pastors in the Church. Ever since then, he had been using diabolical means to deal with me. I remember him coming to my room in the midnight. The Lord told me in the dream that father was about to harm me. When I woke up, I saw him with a black pot and piece of red cloth in his hand. He stood over me...

SCENE FIVE (FLASH BACK)

(Damola is on the bed in his semi dark room, looking at Talimi, wrapped in white cloth, holding a small black pot with a red cloth tied round the edge.)

DAMOLA: *(looks surprised.)* What are you doing, dad?

TALIMI: *(growls in a deep voice.)* You've pushed me too far, son. You'll either be initiated or die.

DAMOLA: *(gets out of the bed to sit down.)* You're not in the position to determine what happens to me. It's either God or I decide that. I have decided to follow Jesus. I'm not turning back. So God decides what happens to me, not you.

TALIMI: I'm your father! You must obey what I tell you.

DAMOLA: There are times in life when one has to make decisions for himself. You decide to join the secret cult.

TALIMI: I didn't decide that, son. My father did. I'm his first child and I was dedicated to the brotherhood long before he died.

DAMOLA: Too bad you allowed him to decide for you. I'm not making the same mistake. No matter what you do, I won't join the cult. You cannot succeed in hurting me in any way because the Bible says that no weapon fashioned against me shall prosper.

TALIMI: Son, you're playing with fire.

DAMOLA: I can choose to play with fire because my father in heaven is the consuming fire.

TALIMI: I'm warning you, son.

DAMOLA: I'm the one in the position to warn you. Dad, if you don't stop this, it can cost you your life.

TALIMI: *(smiles with frustrations.)* We'll see who is dicing with his life.... *(He goes out of the room, looking angry.)*

SCENE FOUR B

(Damola looks round at the rest after recalling the flashback. They are all silent)

SESAN: Going by what you say now, you could be responsible for the death of our father.

YINKA: How can you say a thing like that?

DOLAPO: He may be right, considering the circumstances that surrounded father's death.

DAMOLA: I don't know anything about his death.

SESAN: You could have cursed him to die. You warned him to stop, didn't you?

DIMEJI: *(looks at Damola who looks offended before he stares at Sesan.)* Don't drag the matter. What would you have done if you're in brother Damola's shoes?

SESAN: It's simple. I'll have joined the cult. That would have at least saved the life of our father.

DIMEJI: If you're a real Christian, you won't. I am a Christian. So I won't if I were in brother Damola's shoes. So no one can pick on him or me for that.

DOLAPO: I wish you'll take religion out of this and face the fact. *(She looks at Damola.)* I can see that you don't love our father as I thought despite the position he placed you as the head of everything he has, including the family.

YINKA: *(glances at looks.)* That's not polite of you.

SESAN: Shut up there! You talk of being polite when you're talking of the death in the family. From what mother said about the ghost of our father, there may be more deaths…

DAMOLA: It's okay, Sesan. There would be no more death if we all unite. A house divided against itself cannot stand. **(He looks round at the rest.)** Please, let's give peace a chance. If we keep talking and arguing about this, we wont anywhere. **(He smiles at Sesan who signs and nods silently.)**

BOLADE: *(looks at Damola.)* What do we do about the message of the ghost of your father?

DAMOLA: If at all you see any ghost, it is a demon you see and not our father. The Bible says it is appointment unto all men to die once, after this comes judgment.

SESAN: I have my reservation about that.

DAMOLA: That doesn't matter. What matter is peace in the family. **(There is silence.)** Can we pray now? **(They all close their eyes as he leads them in prayer.)**

SCENE SIX A

(The six members of the brotherhood drive into the compound in six different cars. They park close to the entrance of the house. Their drivers open the car doors for the cult members. All are dressed in black suit over white trousers. They all wear gold chains round their necks. One of the drivers of the car goes to press the door bell. The house maid opens the door)

HOUSEMAID: *(half kneels.)* Welcome, sir.

1ST DRIVER: Is madam Toyeka in the house.

HOUSEMAID: Yes, sir.

1ST DRIVER: *(looks and nods at the rest before he stares at her again.)* We are coming in. Tell her her husband's friends want to see her and her son, Damola.

HOUSEMAID: Pastor Damola is not around, sir. He went to the church.

1ST DRIVER: *(opens the door wider as the members comes out of the car.)* We'll wait for him. *(The men enter. The housemaid hurries towards Bolade's room and knocks at door.)*

BOLADE: *(responds from within.)* Yes?

HOUSE MAID: There are visitors, waiting to see you ma.

BOLADE: Who are they?

HOUSEMAID: They said they are chief's friends.

BOLADE: *(opens the door.)* You mean my husband's... *(The housemaid nods. Bolade hurries to the sitting room where the six members of the brotherhood are waiting. She frowns at them as they stand up.)* H-hello…sirs...

LANDO: *(smiles.)* Hello, madam. Do you remember us?

BOLADE: Yes, sir. You were at my husband's funeral.

LANDO: I guess we are not strangers to you them, are we?

BOLADE: I guess you're not, sir. *(She gestures to the seats.)* Please, sit down and feel at home.

LANDO: Thank, madam. *(He nods at the men to sit. Bolade allows them to sit before she settles on her seat.)*

BOLADE: *(looks round at them.)* What can we offer you, sirs?

LANDO: That would not be necessary, madam .Thank you.

BOLADE: We'll then, what can I do for you?

LANDO: Actually we are here to see you and your first son called Damola.

BOLADE: I see… I hope there's no problem.

LANDO: It's just a little problem we can solve through mutual understanding and co-operation.

BOLADE: Nobody is around now except me and the maid.
LANDO: We were told Demola has gone to the Church. I hope he'll be back soon.
BOLADE: Yes, he may come back soon if he comes straight home after the service. *(She goes to take the mobile phone on the center table.)* I'll call and inform him he has visitors.
LANDO: We'll appreciate that.
BOLADE: *(makes the call and waits for a while.)* Hello... When do we expect you back in the house... No, there's no problem. You have some important visitors... Okay then. We'll expect you soon. *(She looks at Lando.)* He said he'll be here soon. While waiting for him, would you tell me about your mission here, sir?
LANDO: Actually, the detail of the mission is not a subject of discussion with women but I'll tell you a few things which are very vital for you to understand. *(He looks round at the men. Each of them nods at him before he stares at her again.)* There are seven of us in our group. Your husband is the seventh member. Since his death, his heir who happens to be the young man we are expecting is to take his place. If he refuses the position, you may lose all your children. *(Bolade closes her eyes for a while in deep thought, recalling her encounter with Talami's spirit.)*

FLASHBACK

TALIMI: ...The group will pay you a visit very soon. If Damola refuses to occupy the position in the group, there would be deaths and horror in the family...

SCENE SIX B

BOLADE: *(opens her eyes with fright.)* My husband's spirit came to me a few nights ago and told me the same thing.
LANDO: He was supposed to get Damola involved in our group before he died.
BOLADE: From what Damola said, he tried to but the young man had become a religious fanatic.
LANDO: Well, you have a duty now. You must do all you can to make him co-operate with us if you don't want to lose any of your children.
BOALDE: Oh, my God...
LANDO: There's nothing to fear. Do you part and leave the rest to us. *(Outside the house, Damola drives into the premises and frowns at the cars around the place. He hurries into the house. Bolade wears a very impatient looks with all the men looking*

calm and confident. The men stand up when Damola enters the sitting room. Lando smiles at Damola.)

DAMOLA: *(bows.)* Good afternoon, sirs.

LANDO: You're welcome, Damola.

DAMOLA: I was told on the phone that you came here to see me.

LANDO: Yes. We've been talking to your mother and we have to talk to you before we take our leave.

DAMOLA: I see. Please, sirs, have your seats. *(The men again sit down quietly.)*

LANDO: (looks at Bolade.) Madam, you may excuse us now.

BOLADE: *(sighs, stands up and goes to whisper into Damola's ear.)* Damola, this is the moment you have to prove how much you love your family. I want you to do all they tell you. If you don't, there'll be horror and even deaths in the family.

DAMOLA: *(looks puzzled at the men for a while before he looks at her.)* I'll do what is right.

BOLADE: We're counting on you to preserve our lives. Please, don't let us down. *(Damola forces a smile. Then she leaves the sitting room. He goes to sit on her seat and looks at the men indifferently.)*

DAMOLA: What did you tell her that made her so frightened?

LANDO: I told her the truth.

DAMOLA: What do you know about the truth?

LANDO: Young man, we are not here to argue with you or to be interrogated by you. We are here to inform you of your position in the brotherhood. The repercussion of neglecting your position and obligation is what we told your mother.

DAMOLA: *(sighs.)* I guess I don't have the right to ask questions but to listen to you. Okay, fine. I'm all ears.

LANDO: You'll ask your questions later. Before we tell you a few things, we'll like to know what happened to all the things in the secret room of your father.

DAMOLA: *(in a firm voice.)* I burnt the whole shit.

LANDO: That was very daring of you. Did you kill your father?

DAMOLA: No. *(He points at them.)* All of you did when you ask him to do what is not within his power to do. *(All the men look furious but they maintain their peace.)*

LANDO: What is that thing we tried to make him do?

DAMOLA: The same thing which you guys have come for - initiate me into the secret cult. *(He stands up.)* Actually, I don't know why I have to have a round table discussion with you. You're enemies of my family but I don't blame you in any way. It was my father that stoop so low to dine with you.

LANDO: *(smiles.)* Son…

DAMOLA: I'm no son of yours.

2ND MEMBER: That insult is enough!

LANDO: *(glances at him.)* You know the rules. *(He looks at Damola again.)* You must realize that you and other members of your family eat out of the dinner.

DAMOLA: *(snorts.)* How?

LANDO: The group is behind all the financial and other successes which your family enjoys till today.

DAMOLA: That's a lie. My family, including my father knows that through the leading of the Spirit of God, I lead the family in the businesses from the foundation to where they are now. The only role my father played was to give me the authority to run the businesses as I am inspired by God. So don't feel you can come here to take the gory that belongs to God.

LANDO: *(stands up to face him. Damola also stands up.)* We don't strike without a warning. If we are forced to strike, the casualties are always enormous.

DAMOLA: Two of your great weapons are fear and lies. You just used that effectively well on my mother. You threaten to wipe off my family if I don't join you guys in your atrocities. Is that how you fight? I'm your target. Why don't you face me head on. If you really have what it takes to crush me, why not crush me if I give you problem and leave others out of it?

LANDO: We don't fight like that. We do give our potential members time to come back to their senses.

DEMOLA: You must be a very caring group. You're so caring that you can afford to wipe out the family of one of your members just because he failed to carry out an assignment that is too much for him. *(He walked round in front of the men.)* You can go, combine all your forces and fight me. Consider it a challenge. I am ready for you anytime - any day.

LANDO: *(calmly.)* Let's go gentlemen. *(The rest stand up to go.)*

DAMOLA: You know, there's nothing gentle about cult men.

LANDO: *(moves closer to him.)* You just spelt out your doom.

DAMOLA: My father threatened me like that before he died. Let me give you the same warning I gave to him before he was knocked off. You better turn your lives over to Christ otherwise you'll all wind up in the grave like him. *(Lando follows the men out of the sitting* *room.)*

SCENE SEVEN

(Bolade is restless on the bed for a while in the night before she puts on the bedside lamp, takes the mobile phone on the table and makes a call. She waits for a while.)

BOLADE: *(in a whisper.)* Sesan, I want you to see me in my room right now… Don't let anyone see you. *(She puts down the phone and sits on the bed, looking thoughtful. After a while, Sesan knocks at the door gently, opens it and goes inside.)*

SESAN: *(hesitates, looking at Bolade.)* I hope all is well, mum.

BOLADE: I wish it is but it's not.

SESAN: What's the matter? Does it have anything to do with the visit of father's friends which you told us about?

BOLADE: *(nods and gestures to the space beside her.)* Come and have your seat here. *(Sesan goes to sit beside her.)* The situation is worse than the way it was painted. Damola didn't know that I heard all the discussions he had with the men. He insulted them.

SESAN: *(frowns.)* What?

BOLADE: *(nods.)* I fear the worst may happen. I can't help thinking of what the spirit of your father told me and what I heard the men said. They said if I don't persuade Damola to co-operate with them, I may lose all of you, the children.

SESAN: *(sighs and rubs his forehead thoughtfully.)* What are we going to do now?

BOLADE: *(stands up to take a card in a drawer and hands it to him.)* That's the contact address the leader gave me before Damola joined us in the meeting. I want you to see him in the office and ask of the possibility of taking the position of your father in the group since your brother refuses to co-operate with them. *(She sits down again and put her arm round him.)* You're our only hope. Would you save the family from being executed by the group? *(He sighs again before he nods slowly. She smiles.)* Thank you. I know I can count on you.

SCENE EIGHT

(Lando sits on the executive chair in his office, looking thoughtful. Sesan sits in front of him, looking silently at him.)

LANDO: *(clears his throat.)* Yes... It's possible for you to take the position but the first son of the predecessor must be out of the way.

SESAN: What does that mean?

LANDO: To put it in the language you can understand, your brother, Damola must be dead first. *(There is silence as Sesan looks confused, leaning backward on the chair.)*

SCENE NINE

(Damola is the room, sitting behind the reading table and going through some files. Sesan knocks at the door and comes inside, looking jovial. He holds a bottle of wine and two glass cups in both hands.)

SESAN: Hello, brother!

DAMOLA: *(looks at him.)* Hi, Sesan. You look happy today. What's the good news?

SESAN: We won the contract!

DAMOLA: *(look interested.)* Which one of them?

SESAN: The construction of the street drainage that is awarded by the State Government.

DAMOLA: *(looks happy.)* Really?

SESAN: Yes! See! *(He shows him the bottle of wine.)* This calls for celebration, isn't it?

DAMOLA: Yeah! *(Sesan goes to give him one of the glass cups and open the wine. Damola looks the gold ring in his left hand.)* Hey, I don't know you wear ring?

SESAN: *(pours the wine in each cup.)* A friend of mine gave it to me. I want to do him the honors of wearing it for a while before I take it away.

DAMOLA: I see. *(He looks at his drinks.)* I hope the wine is non-alcoholic.

SESAN: I know pastor doesn't take alcoholic so I bought fruit wine.

DAMOLA: *(smiles at him.)* Thank you. Let's pray over it. *(He closes his eye.)* Father, thank you for the contract with the State Government and thank you for the wine. We pray that you perfect what you have started in Jesus' name. Bless the wine and everyone that takes it in Jesus' name. Amen!

SESAN: Amen! *(They both drink the wine.)*

SCENE TEN

(Damola rolls restlessly on the bed at night, holding his stomach as if he feels pain there. He stands up after a while and begins to pray fervently with only his mouth moving. After along time, he runs to the sink in bath room, put one of his fingers into his mouth. He begins to vomit everything in his stomach, including

the wine and Sesan's ring. He feels relieved. When he opens the tap to wash his mouth and face, he sees the ring. He looks stunned.)

SCENE ELEVEN

(Sesan sleeps in his room when the door is knocked gently. It is knocked several times before Sesan wakes up and goes to open the door. Damola enters the room silently and goes to sit on the bed. Sesan who looks puzzled closes the door and moves closer to him.)

SESAN: What's wrong, brother?

DAMOLA: Where did you get the wine you gave to me?

SESAN: I brought it. Why do you asked?

DAMOLA: Are you sure? *(There is silence.)*

SESAN: Yes.

DAMOLA: You better tell me the truth because something strange - something demonic is happening in this house.

SESAN: What is it if I may ask?

DAMOLA: *(opens his fist and reveals the ring. Sesan frantically checks his fingers. The ring is not there. He looks nervously as Damola calmly studies his reaction.)* Are you sure you don't know what is happening here?

SESAN: I... I don't understand.

DAMOLA: If your hands are clean, there's nothing to worry about. If it's not, the wine we drank together will destroy you because it is not an ordinary wine. *(He stands up to go, smiling at his bewildered expressions.)*

SESAN: Wait a minute... Would you at least pray for me?

DAMOLA: I have prayed for you. The only way the prayer can be answered is if you confess what you have done.

SESAN: *(signs.)* Okay.... *(Damola leaves the room. Sesan slowly goes to lie on the bed, recalling the flashback.)*

FLASH BACK (SCENE TWELVE)

(Lando with other six members of the brotherhood sits in the secret room while Sesan kneels down at the centre, holding the bottle of wine in his hands.)

LANDO: ... He has agreed to get rid of Damola before he is qualified to occupy the position of his father. I told him to bring the wine through which we'll release the spirit of bloodshed that will eliminate him.

3RD MEMBER: The release of the spirit of bloodshed is supposed be the last option.

LANDO: Under the circumstances, do we have any other options? *(There is brief silence.)*

4TH MEMBER: I must confess that I am not familiar with the consequences of releasing the spirit of bloodshed.

LANDO; Well, as a way of introduction to the spirit, since you may become a leader of group, the spirit of bloodshed is called Agiri. His mission is to suck the blood of all the enemies we send him to eliminate in the night. There are other spirits at the disposal of the group though, Agiri is the most powerful and ruthless. Although I must admit that Damola is powerful man, going by what he has sone so far but he is no match for Agiri. I am yet to know the person Agiri cannot eliminate. The main reason he is the last option is that we must not make mistake about our victim. Besides, he goes extra mile to eliminate other people that are considered enemies of brotherhood.

4TH MEMBER: I see. If Agiri can do the job we want, why not release him to do it?

LANDO: *(looks round at the men.)* Do we have any objection to that? *(They all shake their heads.)* We'll release Agiri into the bottle of wine. Anyone who drinks it would become his prey. *(He looks at Sesan.)* In other not to raise his suspicion, you'll drink the wine with him. Only two of you must drink it. You'll get rid of the rest if you cannot finish it. *(He takes the ring on the table beside him.)* You'll wear this ring for seven days, the period which Agiri would operate. We don't expect any thing to go wrong but if anything goes wrong, let me know....

(Sesan signs on his bed after he recalls the flashback.)

SCENE THIRTEEN

(Lando is busy, going through some files in his office when the secretary comes in.)

SECRETARY: There's a man who insists that he must see you now. I told him you'll see him when you're through with the work. He said he has urgent message for you.

LANDO: *(looks thoughtful for a while.)* Who's he?

SECRETARY: Mr. Toyeka.

LANDO: You can send him in.

SECRETARY: He met other people who are also waiting to see you, sir.

LANDO: I'll see them later but send Toyeka in right away. *(She leaves the office. After a while, Sesan hurries inside, looking impatient.)* Hello...

SESAN: *(looks a little upset.)* Good morning, sir.

LANDO: The morning doesn't seem good to you, does it? Sit down and tell me the problem.

SESAN: *(sits down at once.)* I'm going through hell right now. *(He shows him his hands.)* I don't have the ring.

LANDO: *(looks shocked.)* What? Why did you remove it?

SESAN: *(impatiently.)* I didn't remove it! After my brother and I drank the wine, everything went well until in the midnight when he came to my room. He asked me where I got the wine we drank together. I told him I brought it. Then he showed me the ring in his hand.

LANDO: *(frowns.)* How did he get?

SESAN: *(looks confused too.)* How am I supposed to know?

LANDO: *(looks thoughtful for a while.)* Did he remove it from your hand?

SESAN: Of course not! I was wearing it in my hand when I slept and there's no way he could have entered my room because the door was locked. In fact, I was the one that opened it for him when he banged at door of my room.

LANDO: Did you ask him to give you back the ring?

SESAN: No.

LANDO: Why?

SESAN: I... I was confused and scared.

LANDO: Listen, son. You must do all you can to get the ring back from him. Having the ring in the hand of an enemy that is so powerful is a bad omen. I can't describe the catastrophe that will come out of it if you don't retrieve it within three days!

SESAN: *(beginning to tremble.)* W-what if I can't?

LANDO: *(looks frustrated as he speaks through his teeth.)* You have to get it by all means because the ring is the means to control Agiri. I honestly don't know what made me trusted you with it. Only the leaders of brotherhood are trusted with the ring for the reason which only the head are privileged to know... *(He robs his forehead thoughtfully.)* I don't know what to tell others but you must understand that your life as well as others depend so much on getting back the ring.

SESAN: *(nervously.)* I'll try and get it.

LANDO: *(looks as if it just occurs to him.)* By the way, you drank the wine and you're not wearing the ring?

SESAN: *(nods.)* Yes... What about it?
LANDO: You're supposed to be a dead man the moment the ring disappears in your hand. *(Sesan looks thoughtful as he recalls his dialogue with Damola)*

FLASHBACK

SESAN: Wait a minute... Would you at least pray for me?
DAMOLA: I have prayed for you. The only way the prayer can be answered is if you confess what you have done....

(Sesan blinks his eyes when he hears Lando's voice.)

LANDO: ...If you don't want to be hit by Agiri, go and get the ring now! *(Sesan stands up clumsily to leave.)*

SCENE FOURTEEN

(Damola, Dimeji, Dolapo and Yinka are in the sitting room. They all have a Bible each)

DAMOLA: The summary of all we've learnt so far are: Salvation is a priceless gift from God through our Lord Jesus. Obedience to the word of God guarantees the blessings of Abraham. Prayers guarantee victories over our enemies and constant feeding on the word of God in the Bible makes us to grow strong and matured in the Spirit. We learnt that everything about our physical, spiritual and eternal lives is determined by how much of the word of God we take on daily basis. If you don't take the Bible as your watch word, the devil can easily disarm and even destroy you. Don't forget that if the devil wants to attack anyone, the first thing he'll do is to take the Word of God from him. We'll not fall prey of the devil in Jesus' name.
THE REST: Amen!
DAMOLA: *(looks round silently.)* I think that's enough for today. Do you have any questions before we pray?
DOLAPO: The question I want to ask may not be in relation to what we just studied. It has to do with mother and brother Sesan. I observed they've stopped gathering with us to pray.
YINKA: Yes. That's true. Brother Sesan's attitude is changed - I mean he seemed bordered by some things.
DIMEJI: Since the question doesn't have anything to do with the fellowship, let's round up...
DAMOLA: It's okay, Dimeji. I'll tell you what's happening. *(He is silent for a while, looking thoughtful.)* A day before yesterday, Sesan

came to me with a bottle of wine to celebrate the contract which he claimed was awarded to us by the State Government. I noticed a ring in his hand as we drank the wine. That midnight, I had a very serious stomach pain. I prayed and vomited everything I've taken that day. Guess what I saw in the vomit. I saw the same ring in his hand. *(The rest looked puzzled.)* I went to his room immediately and asked him where he got the wine he gave to me to drink. He never told me what he was up to until yesterday when he demanded for the ring... *(He looks thoughtful.)*

SCENE FIFTEEN (FLASH BACK)
(Sesan kneels before Damola in the sitting room, begging.)
DAMOLA: Why is the ring so important to you?
SESAN: I'm going to meet the guy who gave it to me soon.
DAMOLA: Tell him or her it's with me. I need it as a testimony in the Church.
SESAN: Please, brother....
DAMOLA: Save your breath, Sesan. I wont give it to you, no matter what you do or say.
SESAN: B-but the ring is mine.
DAMOLA: I understand that but what I don't understand is how it ends up in my stomach.
SESAN: *(frowns.)* It was in.... in your stomach?
DAMOLA: There are things you have to tell me. If you don't tell me, I wont give you.
SESAN: *(touches his head thoughtfully.)* Em... The friend is.... called.... em... kayode. I guess he's into black magic or something like that...
DAMOLA: *(looks firmly at him.)* I wont buy that story. Give me another one. In your new story, link the celebration of the false contract with the ring. *(Sesan stands up in frustration and hurries out of the room.)*

SCENE FOURTEEN CONTINUES
(There is silence for a while.)
DAMOLA: I'm almost sure he's gone to pitch his tent with the cultists.
YINKA: What are you going to do?
DAMOLA: I don't know yet.
DIMEJI: *(in a quiet voice.)* You have to forgive him.
DAMOLA: If I have not forgiven him, I wouldn't have prayed for him. If I have not prayed for him, he would probably be dead by now. Right

now, I'm anxious to bury the issue but the problem keeps growing into monster because he is working against me. I have to know the purpose of that ring and how far he has gone before I consider giving it to him. Going by what he said about his friend who gave it to him, and going by what father tried to do to me to make me join the secret cult, I'm sure the ring is from the cultists. I'm yet to know if the ring is meant to harm me or make me comply with what they want. In any case, he must talk to me if he needs help.

DOLAPO: *(thoughtfully.)* There is no doubt that the ring is meant to harm you.

DAMOLA: I don't want us to jump into that conclusion yet.

YINKA: In any case, it's hard to imagine he can go that far. It's unbelievable that he can prove to be more loyal to the enemies than his own family.

DAMOLA: Forgiveness and prayers are the only ways to bring him back. So let's not hold it against him but we would need him to confess what he has done so far. *(Bolade walks quietly to them. Everybody becomes silent when she comes to join them.)*

BOLADE: *(goes to sit beside Damola. She signs and looks round at them before she fixes her stare at Damola.)* If there's anything wrong in what Sesan has done, I caused it.

DAMOLA: What? You asked him to poison me?

BOLADE: No. His action is actually meant to protect the family, not to kill anyone of you. *(She begins to cry.)* I was scared that those men will cause your deaths… and I don't want to lose any of you. So I told him to contact the group... *(Suddenly she grabs her neck, screaming and looking as if something invisible is holding her neck. Damola quickly holds her. Blood begins to come out from her mouth. The rest begin to shout the name of Jesus.)*

DAMOLA: *(begins to pray fervently speaking in tongues.)* I bind you, spirit of death in the name of Jesus! The Bible says when the enemies come against us like flood, the Spirit of the Lord shall set a standard against them. If this is true, I bind you now in the name of Jesus! *(The rest continues to shout "amen!". As they pray, Sesan enters the sitting room, looking frantic.)*

SESAN: Oh my God! Jesus, help us! *(Damola continues to pray. Sesan joins the rest to shout "amen")*

SCENE SIXTEEN A

(Bolade lies on her bed, sleeping with others round her.)
SESAN: If you have given me the ring, all these would not have

happened. *(The rest looks at him with surprise.)*

DAMOLA: You still have the guts to talk about the ring. *(He moves closer to him.)* If I had not travailed in prayers over you, we'll be arranging your funeral by now. *(Sesan frowns as he recalls his dialogue with Lando.)*

FLASHBACK

LANDO: ... By the way, you drank the wine and you're not wearing the ring?

SESAN: *(nods.)* Yes. What about it?

LANDO: You're supposed to be a dead man the moment the ring disappears in your hand....

SCENE SIXTEEN B

(Damola's voice jerks Sesan back from his thoughts.)

DAMOLA: You think we don't know you've gone to dine with the cultists? *(Sesan frowns. Damola moves closer to him again.)* If you don't team up with your own family by telling us what we need to know, you'll perish with them. I can't keep protecting someone who is head bent at ganging up against the people of God. Now I'm going to ask you for the last time, are you going to tell us the whole truth now? *(There is long silence. Damola shouts, waking Bolade up.)* You have no choice unless you want to wind up in the grave. Are you going to tell us or not?

BOLADE: *(in a quiet voice.)* You have to tell them. *(The rest who do not know she is already awake quickly look at her. She smiles.)* I'm okay now. Jesus just proved that he's more real than what we can see.

DAMOLA: *(smiles.)* Praise God! *(The rest, except Sesan respond by shouting, "amen!")*

BOLADE: I've told them I sent you. It's not your fault. It's mine. So you can tell them what happened.

SESAN: *(kneels down in front of Damola.)* Would you really forgive me if I tell you how far I went. *(Damola pulls him up, smiling at him.)*

DAMOLA: You're my brother. Besides, God does not desire the death of a sinner but to repent. Just tell us what we need to know. We'll trash out the madness of this occult group once and for all. *(Sesan looks round, looking uncomfortable.)* Let's do it this way. Let's go to my room. I'll take the position of a Pastor rather than your brother and listen to your confession. Then we'll pray together. *(He*

smiles at him.) How about that?
SESAN: *(nods.)* Okay.
DAMOLA: *(looks at the rest.)* You can stay here with mother. *(He and Sesan leave the room.)*

SCENE SEVENTEEN

(Lando is holding meeting with other members of the Brotherhood in the secret room.)
LANDO: ... I sense danger coming against us at the double.
2ND MEMBER: Does it have any thing to do with Damola?
LANDO: Yes.
3RD MEMBER: What shall we do about him?
LANDO: We have to wipe him and his family out.
2ND MEMBER: Has it gone that far?
LANDO: Yes. We've been betrayed by his brother, Sesan. He is expected to show up with the ring since he's having problem dealing with Damola.
4TH MEMBER: Is there any other way out?
LANDO: I'm afraid, there is none.
2ND MEMBER: We'll wipe out the entire family then and make room for someone else from another family to join us. I guess that's the rule.
LANDO: Yes. *(He looks round at them.)* We'll wipe out the family tonight. Any objection?
3RD MEMBER: How about the ring.
LANDO: I'll find a way to get it after wiping the family. *(Each of them nods his head in agreement.)* We'll get rid of the family.

SCENE EIGHTEEN

(Sean sits on the couch in the sitting room with his hand supporting his head, looking very thoughtful. Damola comes to join him. He goes to sit beside him.)
DAMOLA: What are you thinking, man?
SESAN: *(signs heavily.)* I'm just thinking of life generally. I just wonder if the price we pay to stay alive is worth it.
DAMOLA: *(smiles at him.)* It depends on which angle you took at it. Actually, the life that is worth living is the life in Christ.
SESAN: *(nods.)* Yeah. If not for Christ in you that was extended to me, I would have died. *(He looks at him.)* Brother, I didn't know Jesus is so real and so powerful until recently.

DAMOLA: *(smiles.)* You have confidence in him now, don't you?
SESAN: *(frowns.)* What? With what has happened so far, only a mad man would doubt that he can deliver people from the devil. As you can see, I'm already a fanatical Christian.
DAMOLA: *(laughs.)* That's the spirit. *(He brings out the ring.)* What do you think we should do with this?
SESAN: I don't expect you to be in possession of that stuff.
DAMOLA: *(smiles.)* All right. I'll destroy it... I don't know if mother told you she wants us to have a night vigil today.
SESAN: Oh, yeah she told me.
DAMOLA: You need to sleep early before then. *(Sesan nods at him. He pats him on the shoulder and stands up to go.)*

SCENE NINETEEN
(The members of Brotherhood gather at the secret room, standing round the shrine as Lando makes some chant.)
LANDO: Agidi, the blood thirsty spirit that fights for those who are his, crushing his enemies in the head without mercy and sucking their blood like water. We call upon you now to come up and be ready to wipe out the family of Toyeka that choose to be our enemies! Come! Come! *(There is lightening, accompanied by thunder. There wind begins to blow violently. The men begin to made soft grunting sound.)* Come! Agidi, the wonder spirit! Come! *(There is smoke and a spirit in the form of a big head with hideous looking face. It makes hissing sound like snakes.)* Welcome, Agidi! We want you to go after our enemies, Toyeka family and wipe out every member. *(The spirit disappears in a smoke.)*

SCENE TWENTY
(The members of Toyeka family, including Bolade are praying fervently with Damola leading them. As they are still praying, there is smoke in the air. Agidi appears in the air like a spectrE.)
DAMOLA: *(prays fervently.)* Every weapon fashioned against us in this family shall not prosper in Jesus name! We command the weapon of our enemies to be turned against them in Jesus' name. The word of God says even though we walk through the valley of shadow of death, we fear no evil become Jesus is with us. If God be with us, who then can be against us! *(He begins to sing.)*

    The Lord that answers by fire
    Let him be my God!

(As he sings, Agidi disappears with the smoke.)

SCENE TWENTY ONE
(The members of the Brotherhood are still in the secret room, making chant. When Agidi appears in their midst in the form of smoke, thunder strikes with lightening. Agidi circles round them. The men begin fall backward, looking as if they are in pain, screaming with pains as blood spill out their bodies. They are thrown against the wall violently until they are all dead.)

SCENE TWENTY TWO
(Sesan watches the television which broadcasts the news about the Brotherhood.)

NEWSCASTER: ...The six men were found dead in the place that looked like a shrine this morning. The cause of their deaths is yet to be ascertained by the police...

SESAN: *(stands up abruptly, looking excited.)* Brother Demola! Everybody, come and listen this news! Our enemies are all dead! *(He hurries inside the room.)*

RITUAL KIDS' KIDNAPPERS

PROLOGUE

(Narrator stands before the audience of children, parents, youths, teachers and other adults with the light beaming at him at the centre stage. He wears a T. Shirt tagged: "Why Involving Children In Cultism?" He looks rather grave and very serious.)

NARRATOR: ... You have probably heard of cultism extending to primary schools. You may also wonder why this is so. This play will explain a few things to you in that respect but before then, I want you to understand the dreadful implications of bringing these young ones into the vice rings.

From the results of the research we have conducted so far, which reflect in this play, multitudes of monsters are in the making if children are introduced into cultism. Of course, one monster would naturally give birth to another by getting others involved. Either as victims or participants, if children are brought into the vice ring and they manage to survive the trauma, more often than not, their consciences are deadened at early stage of their lives, making them to consider human beings as goats or Christmas chicken. We are talking about ritualism and even cannibalism here, not just cultism at the face value.

The information and education you will find in this play is not meant to frighten anyone by explaining the obvious reasons for the missing people in our society but to let everyone understands the reality of life everywhere in the world, including the so-called advanced nations.

There are lots at stake if we shy away from the reality and conclude that this is all about religion. Hence, it better to face it head-on and think of God as the solution to this problem before catastrophe becomes the order of the day.

This play: Ritual Kid's Kidnappers is about mysterious disappearances of people, including school children. The story is based on facts we gathered in the course of research works into cultism at various levels. Putting aside any religious sentiments, the story offers the only way to equip and secure children against these monsters.

Before you sit back, enjoy and educate yourself with this play, I'll sing a song of warning to everybody, especially to children. *(He begins to sing.)*

Watch out, children, watch out, young folks
You're in the world that is full of evils
The evils that abound can destroy you
If you are not a real child of God

Watch out, children, watch out, young folks
You need Jesus to live in your heart
And then tell him everything you need
He will always be there to help you out

Don't be afraid, do not lose your faith
For Jesus Christ will not let you down
Wherever, whenever you go, call upon Him
He is there with you to help and deliver you

(When he finishes singing, he bows. The audience gives a round of applause as he leaves the stage.)

SCENE ONE

(Victor glances through his book in the sitting room. He is sitting beside his father, Ajewole who is reading the newspapers on the couch.)

VICTOR: .... Daddy I need a children Bible .

AJEWOLE: I thought you had one .

VICTOR: I gave it to one of my friends at the Bible Club in the school.

AJEWOLE: Why do you have to do that without first telling me? You know we cant afford giving out Bibles like that. Do you have any idea how much a children Bible cost?

VICTOR: Oh dad! I was trying to do what we were taught at the Bible Club.

AJEWOLE: What were you taught at the club that made you give away your Bible?

VICTOR: We were taught to always share with needy people.

AJEWOLE: Son, if we share the only thing we have with the needy people, we'll also be in need very soon.

VICTOR: No dad! You are wrong. God always blesses those who give to others. *(He takes the book titled "Foundation Bible Club Story Book" in his hand and opens a page to him.)* There is a story in this book which we used at the Club. It's about a boy called David. He gave his friend his spare uniform and God gave him a brand new bicycle!

AJEWOLE: *(laughs.)* So you expect God to give you too a bicycle for giving away your Bible, right?

VICTOR: I expect God to bless me somehow though I don't know how.

AJEWOLE: Okay, son. You win. I'll get you another Bible but don't give it away. If you give it away again, you wont get another one. Do we have a deal?

VICTOR: Yes! Thank you daddy....

SCENE TWO

(Victor, Femi and Kunle are going to school when a car suddenly double crosses them. Three men come out of the car, each of them takes a child. The children try to scream and struggle with them but when they use handkerchiefs to block their noses, they all pass out without any more sound. The men take them into the car and then hurriedly drive away.)

SCENE THREE

{*Victor, Femi and Kunle are driven into the bush. The car stops and the men take the children out to a small hut. There are other children in the room. The children are either sleeping or sitting, looking depressed or frantic. Victor is the only one that is awake among the three children as the men take them out of the car.)*

VICTOR: What are you going to do with us?

1ST MAN: *(points at rest of the children.)* Ask them.

2ND MAN: There were more than this before but most of them had been sold.

VICTOR: Y- you can't sell me! I'm a child of God! *(The men laugh.)*

1ST MAN: Two bad. God just lost another child.

VICTOR: If you don't take us back to where you picked us from, God will fight with you.

3RD MAN: God will fight us? All right, we'll prepare for battle. *(The men walk out and close the door. There are five men keeping watch over the hut.)*

SCENE FOUR

(Victor sits at the centre of the room talking to the few children that are awake while the rest sleep on the floor.)

VICTOR: We've been thought at the Bible Club in my school that the world is full of evil. Many people steal children like us and use them to serve the devil but those who have faith in Jesus Christ will be delivered. We must pray together and then expect Jesus to send down the angels to deliver us. We've heard and read stories in the Bible about how God deliver his children. So we are going to pray that God should get us out of this place. Before then, let's sing one of the songs we were taught at the Bible club. It goes like this:

> From day till night
> I know God is by my side
> From night till day
> I know God will never leave me
> Never leave me….

SCENE FIVE

(Victor and few of other children are singing and clapping in the hut. The guards are fast asleep.)

VICTOR: *(leads others in singing.)*

> He's a miracle working God
> Hallelujah…
> He's an alpha and omega….

Higher, higher
Higher, Jesus, higher….
Winner ooo…
Are you a winner?
I am a winner in the Lord Jesus...

(As they sing, a small light appears through the window. Only victor seems to see it.) Look! *(All the children singing with him look at the direction.)*

FEMI: What's it?

VICTOR: It's a light. *(The rest look again.)*

FEMI: We can't find any light.

VOICE: Victor, my child. I have heard your prayers and praises. I have sent this light to guide you out of the camp of the enemy. You and your friends can follow the light. By this time tomorrow all pain will be over.

VICTOR: *(jumps up.)* Did you hear the voice?*(The rest of the children look puzzle, shaking their heads.)* I think it is Jesus talking to us. He said he has heard our prayers and praises. *(He looks up.)* Thank you. Jesus! *(He looks round at the rest.)* Friends, let's get out of this place. The Lord promised to lead us out of the camp of the enemies.

SEYI: If we try to escape, those men would kill us.

VICTOR: And if we stay here, they'll kill us. It's better we trust Jesus to get us out of this place than to wait till they kill us. *(He looks round.)* Who is going to follow me? *(Only Yomun refuses to follow them. The rest, including those who are once sleeping get prepared to follow Victor who is by the door already. He pushes the door open. He gestures them to keep quiet as they walk slowly and gently pass the guards. They make their way into the bush.)*

SCENE SIX A

(Ajewole, Sarah, Pastor and two other people are praying in the sitting room.)

PASTOR: ... In Jesus name we pray. As God has assured us that the boy is fine, we are going to ask the Lord to bring him home. Let's begin to pray now... *(They continue to pray.)*

SCENE SEVEN

(Yomun waits in the hut for a moment before he stands up. He walks through the door and finds the guards still sleeping. As he

tries to go through the direction the children that escape, he falls down. One of the guards wakes up with a start and looks at him. He frantically stands up and goes to grab Yomun.)

1ST GUARD: *(in a loud voice that startles the rest.)* You! Where do think you're going?

YOMUN: I just come out to warn you that the children have escaped. I'm the only one that is left.

1ST GUARD: *(looks frantic.)* What! Guards! We are in deep shit! *(He looks at the rest who are half awake.)* I was told our products have escaped. *(The rest of the guards quickly enter the hurt while the 1st guard continues to interview, Yomun.)* Where did they go?

YOMUN: I... I don't know...

1ST GUARD: For how long have they gone?

YOMUN: I don't know. It may be an hour ago. I'm not sure. I was sleeping when they left otherwise I would have informed you before now. *(The rest of the guards come out.)*

2ND GUARD: We can still hunt them down. They are just kids. So we can easily track them down.

1ST GUARD: You are right. Let's go, guys. We have to go hunting for them before the boss comes back otherwise, we'll be in big trouble. *(He points at the 3rd Guard.)* You can wait and keep watch over the remaining child. He was trying to escape when I caught him. *(He looks at the other guard.)* Let's go. *(The two guards leave the place.)*

SCENE SIX B

PASTOR: *(continues to pray with others at Ajewole's house.)* Let's pray that the Lord will send his angel to protect the child and bring him back home. Let's pray in the name of Jesus... *(The people begin to pray fervently again.)*

SCENE EIGHT

(The children are in the bush, looking very exhausted.)

SEYI: ...I think we are lost.

VICTOR: No, we are not. There's a light guiding us. I can see it.

FEMI: You're the only one seeing the light. We can't.

VICTOR: I know but I know it's the Lord that is leading us.

KUNLE: *(finds a place to sit.)* Can we rest for a while?

VICTOR: Okay everybody, let us rest. *(They all sit down on the ground. Victor begins to sing. The rest sing with him.)*

My Jesus today...

My Jesus tomorrow
My Jesus forever
He is a wonderful Lord!

(Some of the children sing while some cry. Victor goes round them, patting each of them on the shoulder, still singing.)

We belong to Jesus
We are children of Jesus
He never sake us
He will not let us down!

SCENE NINE

(The 1st guard hears a voice and pauses. He gestures to the 2nd guard to keep quiet. There is a brief silence ahead of them.)

1ST GUARD: *(points at the direction.)* There they are... *(He looks at the 2nd Guard.)* Can you hear them?

2ND GUARD: *(listens briefly and hears the children singing faintly.)* Sure.

1ST GUARD: Let's go and get them. *(As they hurry forward, they hear the sound of a wild animal. The two guards look round them frantically.)* Where does that sound come from?

2ND GUARD: *(in a frightened tone.)* I... I don't know....

1ST GUARD: *(shrugs.)* Let's go before the children know we are around.... *(As they move towards their direction, there is another sound with violent movement round the bush. The guards become rooted to the ground, looking horrified.)* Th-there is ... a ... dangerous animal around here! *(There is another loud noise with violent movement. The guards take to their heels, running and falling over some woods in the bush. The dreadful sound noise continues until they run far away from where they can reach the children.)*

SCENE TEN

(The children are sleeping as the day breaks.)

VOICE: Victor, Victor, it's time to go home now. I've made available a bus that will take you home at the road ahead of you. *(Victor wakes up with a start and begins to sings.)*

From east to west
There is no other God
I know there's no other God

From day till night
I know God is by my side
From night till day
I know God will never leave me
No other God

(The children begin to join him in singing as they leave the place victor continues to lead them in the song.)

His name is higher
Than any other name
His name is Jesus
His name is Lord...
That's why...
He is Lord...
Amen
He has risen from the dead
He is Lord
Hallelujah
Every kneel shall bow
Every tongue confess
That Jesus Christ is Lord...

SCENE ELEVEN

(The rest of the guards are waiting at the hut with Sangolana who looks very angry.)

SANGOLANA: *(looks at guards.)* The children escaped from you and you have the guts to tell me this?

1ST GUARD: We searched the whole forest but we were chased away by wild animals.

SANGOLANA: *(on top of his voices.)* Wild animals?

2ND GUARD: Yes! They are so big. I'm sure they must have killed the children.

SANGOLANA: *(roars with angry laughter.)* You're joking, right? Wild animal killed the children and left you alive?

1ST GUARD: We have to run from them!

SANGOLANA: There are no wild animals around here, you fools! You need a better excuse than that otherwise I am going to have you executed right away.

1ST GUARD: It's true, boss. We heard the voice of wild animals.

SAGOLANA: What am I supposed to believe in you stories? You said you saw wild animals. Now you're saying you heard them. If you see any wild animal, how did they look like? *(There is complete silence as he walks round them.)* We've been operating in this place for years. There are no wild animals here because this is not a forest. Perhaps you want to tell me squirrels are or other bush rats are the wild animals that stopped you from bringing the children that escaped.

2ND GUARD: I swear they are wild animals.

SANGOLANA: Shut up! *(He looks round at the men.)* Listen now all of you. For being so negligent enough to almost all the children in your custody to escape, you'll have to get me twenty children today otherwise, you'll all be dead before you know it....

SCENE TWELVE

(Gabriel who wears white cloths drives a white bus on the road just as the children are getting out of the bush. He stops the car.)

GABRIEL: Hello, children! *(The children look at each other's faces.)* Do you need a drive home?

FEMI: We don't trust strangers, sir, not after what happened to us. We are sorry.

GABRIEL: I'm not a stranger. Your father sent me to take you home. *(He points at Victor.)* You remember what you were told this morning?

VICTOR: *(looks excited.)* Yes! *(He whispers into the ears of the children.)* I think he's the angel the Lord has sent to take us home. Let's go, friends! *(He beings to sing as they enter the bus.)*

> I am a blessed child
> Jesus makes me a blessed child
> I am a blessed child
> Are you a blessed child?

(The rest sing with him as the bus drives away.)

SCENE THIRTEEN

(Ajewole, Sarah and the rest are still praying when Ajewole's phone begins to ring. He goes to pick it.)

AJEWOLE: Hello... Wonderful, Jesus! Where's he? We'll be there in soon. *(He puts down the phone and goes to tell the rest.)* Victor had been found!

THE REST: Praise God!

AJEWOLE: I was told a man took him and other children to the school.

Only two of them are from the school. The rest had been taken to the police station. Let's go and bring him home. Wait... I'll get the key to my car. *(He goes inside.)*
SARAH: *(goes on her kneels, singing tearfully.)*

> Sweet Jesus
> How wonderful you are…

THE WEIGHT OF DEATH

THE VALUE OF LIFE

How can you know the value of your life
If you have not seen how lives are wasted?
How can you know the value of peace in the world
If you do not the price of world war?

What value do you attach to good health
If you have never felt so sick in life?
What value can you attach to food
If you have never felt very hungry?

How can you possibly value your freedom
If you have never been a slave in life?
How can you appreciate the love of God
If the devil never hurt you like Job?

How can you value salvation of your soul
If you don't believe the Word of God?
How can a man value his eternal life
If he does not know the life after death?

Why should a sane man choose to die
When Jesus offers him the chance to live?
Why would anyone rejects Jesus Christ
When he knows the devil seeks to destroy him?

EPISODE ONE

THE REALM OF THE SPIRIT

SCENE ONE
(Awojebe and Awoseun are in the shrine together, talking.)
AWOJEBE: Son...
AWOSEUN: Yes, father...
AWOJEBE: I want to show you how dark the world is. *(Awoseun looks interested.)* You have always heard that the world is full of darkness.
AWOSEUN: Yes, father.
AWOJEBE: Do you know why?
AWOSEUN: I don't know.
AWOJEBE: The reason is that the devil is the king of this world. He is the prince of darkness.
AWOSEUN: That explains why everybody worships him.
AAWOJEBE: It is not everybody that worships him. Those who worship him are the ones that enjoys their lives but those who don't bow to him always suffer. I don't want you to be among those who will suffer. So I want you to always worship the devil. Before you can know why... *(He takes the chain on the shrine.)* I want you to wear this chain round your neck and go into the town and see how the devils torment people of all classes. The chain will give you what we call the third eye through which you can see what is happening in the realm of the spirit
AWOSEUN: *(nods with understanding.)* Okay, Father. *(Awojebe puts the chain round his neck.)*
AWOJEBE: People will not see you as you watch them suffering but you will see them and what causes their problems. *(He makes some incantations as Awoseun disappears.)*

SCENE TWO
(Awoseun appears in the house of Asake and Kola who are sitting and chatting together in the sitting room.)
KOLA: You always look beautiful to me even though you're now a fairly used woman.
ASAKE: Who used me? Is it not you?
KOLA: Yes. You're new when I married you. You'll always be new to

me. *(He stands up.)* Let's go inside the room and fight.

ASAKE: I know you'll suggest that. I'm not ready for that now. *(There is a knock on the door.)* Who is it?

MESSENGER: *(from outside.)* I'm a messenger from Iya Kereku.

ASAKE: You can come inside. *(Messenger comes inside with some bean cakes that are wrapped in some leaves.)*

MESSENGER: Good afternoon, sir, ma.

ASAKE & KOLA: *(at various times.)* Welcome.

MESSENGER: Iya Kereku told me to give you this Akara, bean cakes. She is celebrating the remembrance of her husband's great father's death. So she is giving this to everybody to eat.

ASAKE: *(takes the item from him.)* Thank you very much. Tell her I'll come and visit her later.

MESSENGER: *(bows).* Okay, ma. *(He leaves the room.)*

ASAKE: *(opens the item and takes a piece, eating it.)* This is delicious! Would you like to take some with *gari* for lunch?

KOLA: It's okay. *(Asake places the bean cakes on the table and goes inside as Kola eats out of it slowly. A demon appears and looks at Awoseun who is puzzled to see him.)*

DEMON: *(talks to Awoseun.)* Your father wants you to see me tormenting people that refuse to worship me. I'll show you... *(He points at the Kola as he eats the bean cake.)* The food that man is eating with his wife had been used as a sacrifice to me. Everyone that eats out of it would have problems like poverty, sickness, sorrow, matrimonial or other problems that would make life miserable for them. I am going to make every moment of the lives of this couple miserable.

AWOSEUN: Can I ask you a question, my lord?

DEMON: Yes, go ahead.

AWOSEUN: Why are you doing this to people?

DEMON: That's a good question. I'm doing this because they are my slaves. They refuse to acknowledge me as their lord. When they have problems like this, they will come to me for solution. See you around! *(He disappears. Just then, Asake brings some cassava flakes known as "gari", a bowl of water and two cups.)*

KOLA: *(looks at his gari.)* This is too small for me.

ASAKE: *(in harsh voice.)*That's enough for you, you glutton!

KOLA: *(looks offended.)* Why are you calling me names?

ASAKE: That's not a name. That's the truth. You are the one eating all the food in the house!

KOLA: *(looks furious.)* Your father is the glutton, not me!

ASAKE: *(also looks mad. She slaps his face.)* Goddamn you!
KOLA: *(expresses shock.)* You slap my face? You're a dead woman! *(He pushes her on chair and presses her neck. She screams with pain. Awoseun disappears as he looks concerned.)*

SCENE THREE

(Awojebe is grinding some herbs together at the shrine Awoseun appears in front of him. He stops working and then looks at him.)
AWOJEBE: You're back so soon?
AWOSEUN: Yes, father. I couldn't stand the innocent couple fighting. They are so ignorant of the cause of their problem...
AWOJEBE: You haven't seen anything yet. The way you're reacting shows you know nothing about the dark world. I want you to go to another place and see what is happening there. *(Awoseun again disappears.)*

SCENE FOUR

(Asake lies on the couch while Kola sits close to her.)
KOLA: I am sorry, Asake... *(He tries to touch her.)*
ASAKE: *(pushes his hand away roughly.)* Leave me alone, you murderer!
KOLA: You have the guts to call me names again? After all, you provoked me by slapping me in the face!
ASAKE: *(jumps on her feet and holds him by his cloth.)* Well, finish what you started! kill me! Murderer, kill me!
KOLA: You're provoking me again!
ASAKE: If you don't kill me, I wont let you alone!
KOLA: Now I know you've gone mad.
ASAKE: It is your mother that has gone mad!
KOLA: *(springs up angrily.)* My mother?
ASAKE: Yes! kill me! *(Just then the door bursts open and Pastor comes inside.)*
PASTOR: Mr. Kola, Mrs. Kola, What's wrong?
ASAKE: It's this murderer. He wants to kill me. I promised him if he doesn't kill me, I wont leave him alone.
PASTOR: *(goes to pull them apart.)* Please, let him go. Don't give the devil a chance.
ASAKE: The devil is already in the house!
PASTOR: Even if he is in the house, don't let him take control of your home. **(Asake pushes Kola away.)** Please, sit down and tell me what is wrong. *(She sits down. Kola and Pastor also take their*

seats.)

ASAKE: Someone brought us bean cakes. He told me to get him some gari which I did. He said it was not enough. I playfully told him he eats too much. Before I knew it, he just bounce on me and almost strangled me to death.

KOLA: You're a bloody liar!

ASAKE: You're the liar!

PASTOR: That's enough! *(He looks at Kola.)* You tell me what happened.

KOLA: She was the first to call me names. I insulted her too. Then she slapped me on the face. I got so furious that I bounced on her. That's what happened.

ASAKE: You're the one lying. You call my father names!

PASTOR: It's okay, Madam. *(There is silence.)* Let me ask you: did you actually slap him?

ASAKE: *(turns her eyes away.)* No.

KOLA: Liar! Liar! You look into my face and repeat that.

ASAKE: *(looks at him.)* I did not slap your face!

KOLA: You're a born liar, you know.

ASAKE: *(looks at Pastor, pointing at Kola.)* Did you hear that?

PASTOR: I think the devil has a hand in this matter.

KOLA: The devil has nothing to do with this! She slapped me in the face and I beat sense into her.

PASTOR: Mr. Kola, did you hear yourself? You beat your wife and feel no qualms about that.

KOLA: Now, now, Pastor, I think you're taking sides with her. If your wife slaps you in the face, what are going to do? Give her a kiss and say, "well-done?"

PASTOR: *(looks impatient.)* Listen to me, both of you. The reason you have this problem in your home is that you don't make Jesus the head of your family.

KOLA: Don't bring religion into this. It has nothing to do with it.

PASTOR: Christianity is not a religion. It's a way of life as established by God in the Bible. If you really want to enjoy your life to its fullness, you must be born-again. If you're not born-again, the devil will continue to cause problem.

KOLA: So how do we get rid of the devil that cause the problem? *(He looks indifferent.)* By coming to your church?

PASTOR: I'm not asking you to come to my Church. The Bible says, "seek ye first the kingdom of God and His righteousness and every other thing shall be added unto you." When you seek and get the

kingdom of God by giving your life to Jesus and walking in His ways, you'll have the peace, joy and other blessings you never had.
KOLA: *(still looks indifferent and shrugs.)* Okay.
PASTOR: Shall we pray. *(They bow their heads as he leads them in prayer.)*

SCENE FOUR

(Awoseun appears in the bush, looking round at the place for a while. Then a demon appears and roars with laughter.)
DEMON: Awoseun!
AWOSEUN: *(bows.)* Yes, my lord, the prince of darkness and the king of the world.
DEMON: Have you heard of anything called STD before?
AWOSEUN: Yes, my lord. STD means Sexually Transmitted Disease.
DEMON: Oh no. That's not what I mean. I mean Sexually Transmitted Destruction! I will show you one of the ways I destroy people through sex. I am going to make myself visible while you remain invisible as I perform the operation of mass killings! *(He roars again and changes into a beautiful lady called Emily. She looks at Awoseun and smiles.)*
EMILY: I'm still the same spirit of destruction. I'm beautiful, isn't it? Any man that comes across me is doomed! *(She begins to walk down the road, swaying her hips seductive way.)*

SCENE FIVE

(Kola kneels down in the sitting room, praying loud.)
KOLA: Jesus, if you're real as the Pastor claimed, I want you to bless me with money! Yes! I want you to give me plenty of money. So that I'll be free from poverty. *(Just then Asake comes into the sitting room, looking at him as he prays.)* I also want you to remove the spirit of madness that have entered Asake, my wife! Yes! She behaves like a lunatic! Jesus, turn her into a Zombie that I can control! I command the madness in Asake to disappear in Jesus' name! Amen. *(Asake looks so angry that she grabs him by the cloth and pulls him up.)* Oh, darling, you're back so soon.
ASAKE: Yes, I'm back!
KOLA: Why are you holding my cloths?
ASAKE: *(in angry voice.)* I heard all the names you're calling me.
KOLA: I was praying for you!
ASAKE: I see... Who is having spirit of madness?
KOLA: Oh, no! It's not you I'm talking about...

ASAKE: *(shakes him violently.)* Then who?
KOLA: *(gestures helplessly.)* Em... Em... Someone who told me to pray for her.
ASAKE: Who asks a lunatic to pray for her? Well, I will show you the spirit of madness in this house! *(She pulls his leg until he falls down.)*
KOLA: Asake! Asake! You want to injure me... If I fight you back now, you will say I want to kill you...
ASAKE: I will either kill you or you kill me for calling me a lunatic!
KOLA: Devil, I command you to get out of this house in Jesus' name!
ASAKE: You're calling me devil! You wait for me! I will show you the devil. *(She hurries inside the room. She returns with a cutlass. He flee from the house when she comes out of the room, screaming on top of his voices. She follows him.)*
KOLA: Pastor! Pastor! Somebody - anybody help me! My wife has gone mad again! *(He runs frantically into the street. She pursues him.)*

SCENE SIX

(Emily waits by the road as Otunba drives on the road and stops in front of her. He winds down the car window.)
OTUNBA: Hello, lady!
EMILY: *(walks majestically to him.)* Hi...
OTUNBA: What's a lovely looking lady like you doing around here?
EMILY: I'm going to visit a friend.
OTUNBA: I see. Where is the place?
EMILY: *(points ahead of him.)* Down the road.
OTUNBA: Well, come on in then. I'll take you there if you don't mind.
EMILY: Are you sure you're a gentleman I can trust?
OTUNBA: Oh, sure! I'm a nice guy.
EMILY: *(gets into the car.)* Thanks. *(The car soon drives away.)*

SCENE SEVEN

(Kola runs frantically towards the Church. Asake runs after him with a cutlass. Kola falls down and gets up again until he runs into the Church. He looks round impatiently for the Pastor but it appears there is no one around. When Asake gets closer to the Church, he quickly goes to hide behind the pulpit. Asake looks round for him with anger, throwing away all the chairs on her way. She begins to walk towards the alter. When Kola sees her coming, he takes to his heel again and begins to run round the

church with Asake trying to block his way.)
ASAKE: If I don't cut off your head today, I wont leave you alone!
KOLA: Please, Asake, don't kill me! If you kill me who will be your husband and the father of your children?
ASAKE: I will think about that when you're dead! *(As she draws closer to him, the Pastor enters the church from outside.)*
PASTOR: *(looks shocked when he sees the two of them.)* What is this in the house of God! *(He runs to Asake.)* I command you in the name of Jesus to give me that cutlass! *(Asake stops to look at him. He looks sternly at her.)* I command you in the name of Jesus, the name above every other names to give me that cutlass this minute! *(Asake slowly gives him the cutlass. When he takes it from her, she looks sober and goes on her kneels.)* That's good! Now I know something is wrong with your family.

SCENE EIGHT
(Otunba and Emily are in a hotel room together. He begins to remove his cloths one after the other while Emily smiles at him. Awoseun appears in the room. Only Emily sees him. She waves at him. Otunba looks at what she is waving at and sees nothing.)
OTUNBA: Who are you waving at?
EMILY: Oh, I'm waving at you.
OTUNBA: Well, you can get undressed and let's have some fun.
EMILY: *(sits on the bed.)* Let us talk first.
OTUNBA: *(sits close to her.)* What else do you want to talk about after all the talk. It's time for action.
EMILY: Are you ready to marry me if we have some fun now?
OTUNBA: Yes.
EMILY: How about your wife? Are you going to divorce her?
OTUNBA: Leave my wife out of this, young lady, and let's talk about you and me.
EMILY: If we sleep together now, you understand that we have entered into a covenant which cannot be broken.
OTUNBA: Yes, my dear.
EMILY: Okay, let's do it. *(She stands up to start removing her wrist watch and other things.)*

SCENE NINE
(Pastor is talking with Asake and Kola in the Church.)
KOLA: Pastor, there's nothing you'll say that make me take this woman back into my house.

PASTOR: Remember how all these began. It started when you almost kill her as well because she called you names. So both of you had been used by the devil to cause trouble. *(He takes a Bible and opens it.)* the Bible says in first John chapter 3 verse 8, *"He who sins is of the devil, for the devil has sinned from the beginning. For this purpose the Son of God was manifested, that he might destroy the work of the devil."* In verse 9, we read, *"whoever has been born of God does not sin, for His seed remains in him; and he cannot sin, because he has been born of God."* From this passage, we see that it is only through sins that the devil can have access into your life, your family, your business, marriage and everything that has to do with you. I'll like to tell you at least four out of so many terrible things which sin can do to you.

The first thing sin will do to you is to make you a servant of the devil, going by the passage I just read to you. That means anyone that is not born of God can be used by the devil as he tries to use you to kill each other.

Secondly, if you read the book of Ephesians chapter 5 verse 6, you will see that sin will make God to be angry at you. Anyone that invoke the wrath of God is playing with consuming fire.

According to Ephesians chapter 6 verse 11 to 14, sin will make you vulnerable to the attack of the devil. What I mean by that is that if the devil is not using you to attack others, he will use others to attack you. What has happened so far is a proof of that.

Lastly and more importantly, sin will rob you of the kingdom of God, according to Ephesians chapter 5 verses 3 to 5. Missing the kingdom of God is the worst thing sin will do to you because it will take you to hell.

I will advise you to give your life to Jesus Christ who will make both of you children of God before it is too late. *(He looks at both of them.)* Are you ready to give your hearts completely to Jesus? *(There is thoughtful silence.)*

KOLA: *(nods slowly.)* Yes, Pastor.

ASAKE: I want Jesus in my life too.

PASTOR: Let's pray then. *(He stands up while the two of them kneel in front of him as he begins to lead then in prayers of salvation.)*

SCENE TEN

(Otunba and Emily are on the bed together. She leans on the pillow, facing him.)

EMILY: Since we've had fun, we are now in covenant together.

OTUNBA: Yes, I know.
EMILY: We'll always be together until you're dead.
OTUNBA: What makes you think I'll die before you?
EMILY: I cannot die, you know. *(Otunba laughs.)* What's so funny?
OTUNBA: Only spirit cannot die.
EMILY: You're right. I am a spirit. That's why I can't die. *(He laughs again.)* You don't believe me.
OTUNBA: No, I don't.
EMILY: Well, let's see... *(She changes into a demon. Otunba screams with shock.)*
DEMON: *(roars with laughter.)* You just made a covenant with spirit of death! If you don't die, I wont leave you alone! *(Otunba springs from the bed with only shorts and frantically runs out of the room.)*

SCENE ELEVEN

(Otunba runs out of the hotel to the street, moving from one place to another until he gets tired, panting and walking unsteadily. Emily appears in front of him. He takes to his heel again and goes to a shop.)

OTUNBA: *(pants heavily.)* Water... I want to buy some water...
SELLER: *(comes out of the shop.)* We don't sell water here.
OTUNBA: Please, give me any type of water I can drink. *(As she goes inside, Emily appears. Otunba takes to his heel, going towards a river that is nearby. He gets close to the river and jumps inside. He gets himself drowned inside the water.)*

EPISODE TWO

THE SOUL TORMENTOR

SCENE ONE

(Awojebe and Awoseun are in the shrine together, talking.)
AWOSEUN: Father why is the king of this world tormenting the people?
AWOJEBE: It is because he is the god of the world. He wants people to bow to him. Anyone who refuses to bow would be in big trouble.
AWOSEUN: Is he the supreme God, father?
AWOJEBE: I don't think so but he rules this world.
AWOSEUN: Whoever is the supreme God is not interested in this world.
AWOJEBE: You're right. The supreme God recognizes the fact that this world belongs to Satan.
AWOSEUN: I see. I now understand why we need to worship Satan.
AWOJEBE: I want you go and see what is happening in other places. *(Awoseun disappears.)*

SCENE TWO

(Ibunkun is sitting down dejected, looking as if she would cry. Awoseun appears in the room. The demon also appears almost at the same time.)
DEMON: *(looks at him.)* Awoseun, here is another lesson you must learn about the king of this world. Do you see the woman sitting here...?
AWOSEUN: Yes, my lord.
DEMON: She is under the attack of my servant called spirit of poverty. The messenger caused the death of her husband and left her with three children to cater for. You'll see what is going to happen. *(The demon disappears almost immediately. After a while, two children come into the room, looking sad. They sit at each side of Ibunkun.)*
1ST CHILD: Mummy, I'm very hungry.
2ND CHILD: I'm also very hungry. Can we go and steal some food?
IBUNKUN: Oh, no! Stealing is bad.
1ST CHILD: But we are hungry!
IBUNKUN: If you're caught, you'll be in trouble. *(There is a bang on*

the door.) Who wants to break the door?

LANDLORD: *(from outside.)* Let me break the door, you bloody debtor! The house belongs to me!

IBUNKUN: *(jumps on her feet.)* It's the landlord. *(She goes to hide behind the chair.)* Tell him I'm not around. *(1st child goes to open the door. The children greet Landlord as he enters.)*

LANDLORD: Reserve the greetings till another time. *(He looks round.)* Where is your mother.

1ST CHILD: She's not around, sir.

LANDLORD: She's not around, eh? The person I heard her voice just now is not around, eh. *(He points at the child.)* At your age, you're already a professional liar! You'll soon graduate into a thief. Then you'll become an armed robber! *(Ibunkun springs up from behind the chair.)*

IBUNKUN: That's enough, baba! Haba!

LANDLORD: They would turn into armed robbers because you're teaching them to be professional liars.

IBUNKUN: My children would not turn into armed robbers. If you curse them to become armed robbers, you'll sell your house and they'll rob you of the money.

LANDLORD: *(looks surprised.) Epe*, curse! It's okay. I want you to pack out of my house this minute! You can keep all the money you owe me. Go and use it to look for another apartment. *(He waves angrily.)* Just pack all your rubbish out of my house and allow better tenant to take the room!

IBUNKUN: Baba, landlord, why are you behaving like this now? I told you I will pay all the money I owe you.

LANDLORD: You have been telling the same story. "I'll pay you, I'll pay you" but you never pay anything! I told you that you can pay me in kind but you refuse. Since there is no other way you can pay, I have to forgive you the debt and ask you to pack out of my house - now!

IBUNKUN: Did you offer me another way I can pay you?

LANDLORD: *(snorts.)* You mean you've forgotten or you're just pretending as if you don't understand me?

IBUNKUN: Let's assume I've forgotten or I don't understand.

LANDLORD: You want me to remind you in the presence of your children?

IBUNKUN: *(looks at the children.)* The two of you can go outside and play.

1ST CHILD: We're hungry, mummy. We need food not play.

LANDLORD: *(looks surprised again.)* You mean this children have not eaten.

IBUNKUN: *(looks sad and quiet.)* Yes.

LANDLORD: See what I mean... Eh... *(He shrugs, takes some money out of his pocket and gives it to the 1st child.)* You go to Iya Muraina and buy bread and beans. You can eat it there. Don't border coming back for a long time. Your mother and I have something very important to discuss in private. *(The children looks very happy.)*

1ST 2ND CHILD: Thank you, Baba.

IBUNKUN: *(looks at the children.)* Don't spend the whole money. Reserve some for the evening.

LANDLORD: Leave them alone. Let them spend everything. I have some more to give you if only you will dance to my music. *(He looks at the children.)* You can go, children. *(The children leave the room. He goes to sit down on the bed.)* Come and sit with me here.

IBUNKUN: Baba landlord, I told you I can't do this. I don't want your wife, the Edo woman to come here and dismantle every part of my body me with cutlass like cow meat.

LANDLORD: You don't have to worry about her. You just come and sit down here. *(She reluctantly goes to sit beside him.)* You see, my dear, if the two of us can be together as lovers, I'll take care of you look... *(He brings out money from his pocket.)* Take this... *(She slowly takes it from him.)* Instead of taking anything from you, I'll be the one giving you. All I need from you is for us to be playing together as lovers.

IBUNKUN: You're taking advantage of my condition.

LANDLORD: Oh, no! Not at all.

IBUNKUN: Why don't you just help me without taking anything from me?

LORDLORD: Don't talk like that. You know very well that we're helping each other. When my blood get hot - I mean really hot, you will cool it down for me.

IBUNKUN: You can always ask your wife to cool it down for you, can't you?

LANDLORD: She's already old.

IBUNKUN: I am not a young woman too. You know that.

LANDLORD: You're not, at least not as old as her... Please, let's not talk about my wife again. *(He looks round.)* Where do you want us to bring down the pressure now?

IBUNKUN: What do you mean? We can't do anything here. My eldest child, Lanre will soon come back from the church. You have to arrange another place for us to meet.

LANDLORD: Okay, okay, that's a good idea. *(He stands up.)* I'll arrange a room in my house at Ajilomo street. That'll be our meeting place. I'll come for you when I'm ready. Before you spend all the money I just gave you now, I'll give you more.

IBUNKUN: Okay. Thank you.

LANDLORD: See you later. **(He waves at her and leaves. Awoseun who watches them disappears.)**

SCENE THREE

(Lanre is with Pastor in the church, talking.)

LANRE: Pastor, ever since I've lost my father, life is getting more and more difficult. We have huge debt to settle. Getting common food to eat is a real problem. I have to forgo my admission to study Civil Engineering at University because there is no one that can sponsor me. I tried looking for job so that we can have a steady source of income for my family but I couldn't get any. I pray and pray but God seems so distant from me. I wonder if there is any sin in my life that makes God not to hear me.

PASTOR: Oh, no, Lanre. If at all there is a cause for all these problems, it is not by you.

LANRE: Why are we suffering? God could favour my family because of me. I mean I serve God with all my heart.

PASTOR: I known, Lanre. I know. *(He takes his Bible, looks at it briefly before he stares at him.)* First of all I want you to understand that this world is a battlefield. We have an enemy that is good at using anything - everything in this world, including our flesh to fight us. There are various spirits that fight us because we are Christians. There are spirits of poverty, sickness, pains, sorrow, fear, doubt, lust of the flesh and a whole lot of others. I am also facing a lot of problems too but I know that when we are going through all these, the devil target only one thing in our lives. That thing is salvation of our souls through Jesus Christ. It is the priceless and the greatest gift in life. *(He opens the Bible.)* Let me give you just five reasons you must not let go Jesus out of your life, come what may. One of the reason is found in John chapter 3 verse 16 which makes us realize that Jesus is our only hope out of eternal destruction of mankind.

Secondly, if you let Jesus go out of your life, you have chosen the devil to rule over you.

Another reason you must not let go Jesus is found in Psalm 27 verses 1 to 3 which makes us to understand that the enemies will be chasing you instead of you chasing them. The fourth reason is that the problems will begin to increase instead of reducing. And lastly, if you forsake Jesus, you have forsaken your eternal, spiritual and physical security in life. We have the chance, in spite of all these problems to ask for God's mercy and favour in your family. We'll pray now and then expect miracle later.

As for the food you need in your family, I'll ask the Church to get your family some food stuff. I'll talk to some church members and see which of them can help you get a good job. I'm sure with prayers, we'll get solution to the problem.

LANRE: *(bows before him.)* Thank you so much, sir. I'm really happy and blessed to have you as my Pastor.

PASTOR: All glory and appreciation belong to Jesus. *(He stands up.)* Let's pray. *(He begins to pray.)*

SCENE FOUR

(Ibunkun and the two children are room, talking.)

1ST CHILD: Mummy, I didn't know Baba landlord is nice.

IBUNKUN: Yes, he's nice but, whatever he's given us, he's going to get it back from me.

2ND CHILD: You mean he borrowed us the money?

IBUNKUN: Yes. One way or the other, I'm going to pay him back.

1ST CHILD: How?

IBUNKUN: You don't have to worry about that. *(Lanre opens the door and comes inside, holding a bag.)*

LANRE: *(bows.)* Good afternoon, mum.

IBUNKUN: You're just coming from the Church since?

LANRE: Yes. *(He goes to sit down, putting the bag on the table.)* I had a meeting with Pastor. I told him about our condition. He promised to do something. The Church gave us all these. *(The two children quickly open the bag to see what is inside.)*

1ST CHILD: It's yam, oil, rice and beans... and... What's this?

LANRE: Be careful with that. They are eggs.

2ND CHILD: Eggs! Wao!

IBUNKUN: *(shakes her head sorrowfully and sighs.)* Oh, Lord...

LANRE: *(looks at her with a frown.)* What's it, mum?

IBUNKUN: Is this how we'll continue to live? We've been living on the generosity and mercy of other people.

LANRE: Oh, no, mum... this affliction is just for a while. Very soon, when I get job, I'll be able to take care of everybody and pay our debts, including the house rent.
IBUNKUN: The landlord was here. He wants the house rent paid to him at once.
LANRE: I'll go and appeal to him.
IBUNKUN: You don't have to border. We reached a compromise.
LANRE: He has agreed to give us time to pay?
IBUNKUN: *(looks indifferent.)* Yes.
LANRE: Praise God then. This must be a miracle.
IBUNKUN: Miracle in deed.

SCENE FIVE A
(Landlord packs the car close to a house beside the road. He comes out with Ibunkun at the other side of the car. He carries a nylon bag with him as he winds up the class. Ajoke who is across the street looks at them as they walk into the house. She tails them as they stop by the second door, she hurries out of the place. She waits by the road, waving at commercial motor bike riders. One of them stops. After inaudible dialogue with the rider, she mounts the bike. The rider drives her away. Landlord holds the door open and gestures Ibunkun to enter. She reluctantly enters inside. Landlord follows her and places the nylon bag on the table while Ibunkun looks round the room thoughtfully. Landlord unpacks some oranges out of the nylon bag with a knife. He slices the oranges and begins to suck it.)
LANDLORD: *(gestures to the bed.)* You can have your seat over there. *(Ibunkun goes to sit down slowly. He gestures at the oranges on the table.)* Do you need some? *(Ibunkun shakes her head slowly.)* Why? You don't like oranges? *(She shrugs.)* Fruits are good for the body. When you want to do some exercises like the one we are about to do, you'll need it for energy. I hope you're as strong as you used to be when you were a teenager?
IBUNKUN: I'm as old as your wife, you know that.
LANDLORD: *(laughs.)* I know you say that so that we can do it softly. There is no way you can be as old as my wife. I am sure you'll not act old when I bounce on you.

SCENE SIX
(Ajoke drives through the street to a compound. When the bike stops, she pays the rider. Just then Lydia comes out of the

house, carrying holding a bag.)
LYDIA: Ajoke.
AJOKE: Where are you going?
LYDIA: I'm going to the market to buy some food stuff.
AJOKE: We have to go somewhere now. *(She looks at the bike man.)* Can you take the two of us to where you picked me?
BIKE MAN: Why not?
LYDIA: *(frowns at her.)* Where are we going?
AJOKE: I'm taking you to where your husband is having a nice time with one of your tenants.
LYDIA: Ewo! It's not possible!
AJOKE: Let's go and see. *(They mount the bike and drive away.)*

SCENE SEVEN

(Lydia points at Landlord's car, looking furious. After the bike rider stops behind the car, she pays the bike man who takes off. Ajoke leads Lydia towards the house and points at the second door, waiting while Lydia walks towards the place. She pauses for a while, listening to the conversation going on in the room.)

SCENE FIVE B

(Ibunkun is still sitting on the bed while Landlord sucks the orange, sitting on the edge of the table.)
IBUNKUN: Why are you telling me all these nasty things about your wife?
LANDLORD: It is because it is true! When I married her, she was full of life and beauty. Now that she's become old and unpleasant on the bed. *(Outside the room Lydia put her arms on her head, looking mad with rage.)*
IBUNKUN: You know I'm a descent woman. You're taking advantage of my desperate need of money.
LANDLORD: Oh, come off it again! I told you we are only trying to help each other. You will cool down my pressure and I'll meet your needs. Besides, you also need a man to service you from time to time.
IBUNKUN: I don't need that kind of service. All I need is financial help. If not for that, you know I wont be here.
LANDLORD: Okay, okay, enough of talk, talk. It's time for action. *(He looks at the door.)* Let me lock the door in case of intruder. *(When he goes to close the door, Lydia bursts it opened, dangerously smiling at him. Ibunkun springs on her feet when she sees her.*

Landlord looks so stunned that he is speechless.)
LYDIA: Who has become old and unpleasant on the bed?
LANDLORD: We're talking about somebody else.
LYDIA: I heard everything both of you said! I'll prove it to you I'm not. *(She suddenly pushes him on the bed.)* It's me and you today. You either kill me or I kill you for what you said! *(She looks at Ibunkun who shivers with fear.)* You... I'll spare you for just one reason. He's taking advantage of your condition.
IBUNKUN: *(looks a little relieved.)* Thank you, ma...
LYDIA: Now, get out! *(Ibunkun takes her handbag and runs out of the room, running past Ajoke who is outside the room.)*
LANDLORD: Please, Lydia. Let's go and settle this at home peacefully.
LYDIA: You talk of peace at home when you shamelessly cheat on me and insult me... Insult with injury! Who can take that, eh? *(She walks to the door and locks it, dropping the key between her bosom. A demon and Awoseun appear at the same time in the room.)*
DEMON: *(talks to Awoseun.)* Watch me terminating this man's life.
AWOSEUN: *(looks concerned.)* Why must you do that?
DEMON: It is because it is my job to steal, to kill and to destroy.
LYDIA: *(talks to Landlord.)* I said you either kill me or I kill you.
LANDLORD: *(stands up from the bed, glaring at her.)* I'll rather kill you in self defense than to let you kill me! Open that door before something really bad happens to you now!
LYDIA: I want that bad thing to happen! *(Demon directs landlord to hit her with his hand. Soon they begin to fight. Landlord pushes her on the bed and begin to punch her on the face. There are bangs on the door.)*
LANDLORD: *(screams.)* Give me the key to the door before I kill you! *(Demon points at Lydia and then at the knife that is beside the orange on the table. She looks at the knife and rushes to take it. She stabs him on the chest. Blood gushes out. He goes down on his kneels slowly before he falls down on his face. Lydia looks horrified. She screams with horror.)*
LYDIA: I've killed my husband!
DEMON: *(looks at Awoseun who looks horrified.)* Mission accomplished. *(He disappears.)*

SCENE EIGHT
(Ibunkun looks worried as she walks hurriedly down the street to

her home. She pauses on the way once in a while, looking upward thoughtfully, shaking her head before she proceeds. Lanre and the two children at home, eating gari and peanuts. She opens the door and enters, going to sit down on a chair.)

LANRE: You're welcome, mum.

IBUNKUN: Thank you. *(She looks at the other children.)* The rest of you don't know how to greet?

CHILDREN: We are sorry. You're welcome.

LANRE: Can I get you your own food?

IBUNKUN: *(waves impatiently.)* No.

LANRE: *(stares at her for a while.)* Is something wrong, mum?

IBUNKUN: Did I tell you something is wrong? Better shut up and leave me alone!

LANRE: *(in a quiet voice.)* I'm sorry, mum.

IBUNKUN: *(glances at him as he looks hurt. She suddenly burst out sobbing. Everybody looks confused.)* Why is my life like this? And God is up there, looking at us as bad things happen to us. We have no food, no money - nothing except problems and debts! *(She points upward.)* God, you're far from being merciful!

LANRE: *(looks shocked.)* What!

IBUNKUN: *(glares at him.)* You better shut up there!

LANRE: But, mum, why are you saying all these? God is merciful and faithful. We all know that. He gives us food, good health and protection. A hymn says if we count the blessings God has given us one by one, we'll be surprised what the Lord has done. If we think of what He has not done or what we lack, that's when we'll be ungrateful. If we complain that we have no food, let's think of those who have food but have no appetite because they are sick. If we think of those who are in prison or hospital. If we..

IBUNKUN: I say keep quiet! If we are in prison or hospital, at least, they will feed us there. *(The door is knocked. He goes to open the door. Two men enter the room.)*

1ST MAN: Hello, everybody.

LANRE: Good afternoon, sir.

2ND MAN: *(looks at Ibunkun.)* Are you Mrs. Ibunkun Ilaran?

IBUNKUN: Yes, sir.

2ND MAN: Your attention is required at the police station.

LANRE: *(looks agitated.)* What for, sir?

1ST MAN: *(looks at Lanre.)* And who are you, young man?

LANRE: I'm her first child. *(He waves at the children.)* These are her other children. Is there any problem, sir?

2ND MAN: Well, she is needed for interrogations in connection with the death of Mr. Toyindola who we believe is your landlord.

IBUNKUN: *(jumps on her feet frantically.)* What? He's dead?

1ST MAN: You mean you don't know he's dead?

IBUNKUN: Of course not!

2ND MAN: You were at the scene of his death.

IBUNKUN: I don't know when or where he... He was killed... I mean I was with him when his wife met us in the place but I don't know when he was killed! Please, believe me, I don't know anything about his death....

2ND MAN: You have to come with us. When you get to the police station, you can explain yourself. *(There is thoughtful silence.)* Shall we go, madam?

LANRE: *(recovers from the surprise.)* I'll go with you.

IBUNKUN: *(looks confused.)* Wait behind and look after the children.

LANRE: I have to know where they are taking you to so that I can get some help from the Church. *(Suddenly, the children begin to cry. Seeing them crying, Ibunkun and Lanre begin to cry as they follow the men.)*

EPISODE THREE

THE UNSEEN TORMENTOR

SCENE ONE

(Awoseun is with Awojebe at the shrine.)

AWOSEUN: To be honest, Baba, I don't think I enjoy any of the things you expose me to.

AWOJEBE: All you've seen so far are not for enjoyment but for education. Now tell what you have seen so far.

AWOSEUN: I've seen more than enough to drive me crazy. I've seen the end of a man that entered into a covenant with a demon that appeared like a woman. *(He looks thoughtful, recalling Episode 1, scenes 6, 8 and 9.)* I've also seen how a man was killed by his wife and implicated an innocent woman who was trying to make all ends meet.

AWOJEBE: Let me correct you of a notion. There is no one who is innocent. Secondly, all you've seen so far are child's play.

AWOSEUN: Did you see what I saw?

AWOJEBE: Of course, I've seen worst. Through the chain I gave you I'm able to see what you've see and much more. In fact, that woman you call innocent is coming to me for solution to her problem. When she comes, she would be initiated into the fold of the king of the world through a sacrifice.

AWOSEUN: How are you going to do that?

AWOJEBE: I wont be the one to architect it. The king of the world would do that. You'll see.

SCENE TWO

(Pastor stands in front of a few people who are sitting down, holding publications and tracts in their hands.)

PASTOR: Before we go on evangelism today, I want to briefly explain three ways through which God uses us as his vessels. In Second Corinthians chapter 3 verses 2 and 3, the Bible says that we are epistles which are known and read by all men. It is not written with ink but by the Spirit of the living God, not on tablets of stone but on tablets of flesh, that is of the heart. In other words, your life must reflect the word of God which we preach. When you live by the word of God, people will see it and may be influenced to follow Christ. Hence, God can use your lifestyle that is in conformity with this word to preach to people.

The second way is in Mark chapter 16 verses 15 and 16 where Jesus, our Lord gave us the command that we should go and preach to everybody. When we preach the Gospel to people, God is using us. He's going to use everyone of us in Jesus' name.

THE REST: Amen!

PASTOR: *(raises the publications up.)* These publications are made available by some people who bought them from the publisher. I can assure you that each of them is rich with the word of God and powerful testimonies that can transform lives. We are going round the town, including some schools, campuses and give them the publication. There are some for children, youths and adults. Everybody must be reached with these publications. As you give them, you're preaching the word of God.

You see, if we don't preach the message of Christ, other people will preach message of spirits of anti-Christ to the people. Through anti-Christ messages, many people will go to hell. On the day of judgment, God will ask us, "what do you do to warn the people about hell?"

Quickly, let's us see the third way God can use us as vessels in James chapter 2 verse 17. *(He opens the Bible and begins to read.)* It says, "Thus also faith by itself, if it does not have work, is dead." *(He looks round at the people.)* Your faith in Jesus is proven by your works. When you see fellow believers in need, you need to minister to their needs by giving them what you can afford to give them. The deed is work of faith in God. When you spend your money on the gospel, you also prove your faith in God through works. Any believer who has no works to prove his faith in God is probably an hypocrite. It is like a tree that brings no fruit. Jesus Christ said such tree deserve to be cut down and thrown into fire. It is a crime, therefore, if you don't bear fruits. I want you to stand on your feet now as we pray before going out to fish for souls. *(The rest stands up.)* Tell God that He should make you a productive child of God. *(The people begin to pray. As they pray, Lanre comes inside, looking frantic. He goes to tap Pastor and whisper something into his ears. The pastor gestures him to hold on.)* In Jesus' name we pray!

THE REST: Amen!

PASTOR: I am being told now that brother Lanre's mother is in police station for the offence she knows nothing about. Let us pray that God delivers her in Jesus name. *(As they pray, Pastor gestures* *at one of the people to come forward. He whispers something into his ears before he and Lanre leave the Church. The brother takes over in leading the people in prayer.)*

SCENE THREE

(1st and 2nd children are in the room, looking sorrowful. 2nd child begins to cry while the other cuddles him. After a while, the door opens. Lanre, Pastor and Ibunkun enter the room. As soon as the children see their mother, they jump on their feet and go to hug her. Ibunkun tearfully embraces them, holding them tight. The rest take their seats. After a while Ibunkun also takes her seat.)

LANRE: *(looks at Pastor.)* What can we offer you, sir?

PASTOR: Never mind, my brother. *(He looks at Ibunkun.)* We really have to talk, ma.

IBUNKUN: *(nods slowly.)* Yes, sir. I know.

PASTOR: It's about time you give your life to Jesus Christ so that you don't get into this kind of trouble again. You can feel the pain, the disgrace and the sorrow you caused yourself and everybody.

IBUNKUN: But, Pastor, what is wrong in getting help from the man that promised to help?

PASTOR: The condition he attached to the support is not what anyone expects you to accept. See the whole scenario as it went. He promised to help if you meet him in a house. You went there and the next thing was to see his wife coming to kill him for whatever reason.

Few hours ago just before your son came to the Church to inform me that you were in trouble, I was telling the people how God uses people as vessels. You have to understand that the devil also has a way of using people as vessels as well. He can use what we say or do or think to torment us or other people. He uses our flesh a lot. Everybody is vulnerable. Look, the devil is like a thief who wear different kinds of cloths for operations against mankind. The cloth he uses to steal is different from the one he will use to kill before he destroys the soul completely in hell! The cloths are the human beings. You have allowed the devil to use the landlord to steal your dignity and respect as a descent woman while his wife allowed the spirit of anger to use her to kill him. Unless we are born-again and filled with the Spirit of God, we can never overcome the devil who is determined to destroy humanity.

IBUNKUN: *(looks sorrowful.)* But, Pastor, what are we going to do about our condition now?

PASTOR: All we need to do is to pray and have faith in Jesus who is more than able to help you. If you see the problem as a thing that is bigger than what God can handle, then it will overcome you. *(He pauses for a while.)* Right now, we are doing all we can to get your son a job. Before then, the Church will be giving you the little we can offer you. You will understand that there are many people who have similar problems. But I believe that when your son gets a good job, your family will join the group of givers instead of taking from the Church. *(He stands up.)* Let's pray. *(He prays briefly. When he finishes, he waves at them moving towards the door. Lanre follows him while Ibunkun looks thoughtful.)*

SCENE FOUR

(Ajoke walks in the street, going towards Ibunkun's house. After a while, she knocks at the door.)

IBUNKUN: *(hesitates to stand up from where she sits alone. There is another knock.)* Who is it?

AJOKE: It's me, Ajoke.

IBUNKUN: *(goes to open the door.)* Good afternoon, can I help you?

AJOKE: Now don't treat me like a visitor. Am I not the one who bailed you out of your problem?

IBUNKUN: *(frowns.)* How?

AJOKE: I was the one that confirmed your story that you were not there when the landlord was killed. In fact I told the police it was his wife that killed him with a knife. That's the reason the police let you out of the hook so easily.

IBUNKUN: So what do you want from me?

AJOKE: Wont you let me in? *(Ibunkun shrugs and leads her to a seat. closing the door. Ajoke goes to sit on the chair. Ibunkun goes to sit beside her.)* When I heard what made you fell for the landlord, I felt pity for you.

IBUNKUN: I don't need anyone to pity me. All I need is solution to my financial problem. Right now I'm living by the generosity of other people. *(Ajoke looks thoughtful as a demon appears beside her.)*

DEMON: You must advise her to go to a witch doctor for solution to her problem. *(Then he disappears.)*

AJOKE: What I would advise you is that you should consult a witch door because your problem is not ordinary.

IBUNKUN: But I'm a Christian. I can't go to a witch doctor.

AJOKE: *(smiles at her.)* Well, let's not be hypocritical about Christianity now. To start with, many of the Pastors you see patronize witch doctors. Secondly, we all know it's not possible to practice Christianity alone without adding something with it.
IBUNKUN: But my son, Lanre is a good Christian though I may not be a good one.
AJOKE: Let's leave the issue of good or bad Christians out of it. I just want to tell you that if you don't find solution to this problem of yours, it will embarrass you the more. Already, you've made a name for yourself. So you must do something about this. *(She stands up to go.)* I'll see you again. *(Ibunkun nods thoughtfully.)*

SCENE FIVE A
(Lanre and some church members go round the street, giving out tracts to everyone they meet. Ajoke walks towards them. When Lanre sees her, he hurries to go to her.)
LANRE: Good afternoon, ma
AJOKE: Hello... What's that they call you?
LANRE: Lanre, ma.
AJOKE: Oh, yes. You're my friend's tenant, right?
LANRE: Yes, ma. Thanks for helping my mother the other day.
AJOKE: Thank God. *(She looks around.)* So what are you doing around here?
LANRE: We are doing some evangelical works. *(He brings out the publications and gives copies to her. She looks at them one after the other.)*
AJOKE: *(reads each title.)* What Is The Gain In The Grave?... Life Is A Vapour... The Two Good Friends...
LANRE: Two of them are for children and youths, ma.
AJOKE: *(studies them.)* They are for sales, I suppose.
LANRE: Not really, ma.
AJOKE: Are you sure of this?
LANRE: Actually, they had been paid for by someone.
AJOKE: Why would anyone pay of anything? I thought salvation is for free.
LANRE: Yes, ma, but it cost money to print the publications. It is meant to be given out for free because the Church has paid for the copies we are using for evangelism right now.
AJOKE: If you ask me, I would say there is no sense in this. Why can't the Church give you the money that was used to print all these? You could use the money to feed instead of buying things that has no

value.
LANRE: All of them are valuable, ma. If you read them, you will understand what I mean. They are meant to teach things of eternal values. The Bible says man should not live by bread alone but by every word that proceeds from the mouth of God.
AJOKE: You've been programmed like the rest of the religious fanatics, haven't you?
LANRE: *(frowns.)* I don't understand what you mean, ma.
AJOKE: You could do something better with your life than going about, wasting your time, distributing these. *(She waves the publications.)* You know time is not only money but your life. You can't afford to waste it like this.
LANRE: But it's the work of God, ma.
AJOKE: That's what I mean by saying you've being programmed. Your poor mother and siblings are at home, feeling hungry while you waste your time distributing these in the name of religion. *(Lanre looks thoughtful as there is flash back in scene three.)*

FLASHBACK IN SCENE THREE

PASTOR: ... You have to understand that the devil also has a way using people as vessels as well. He can use what we say or do or feel to torment us and other people. He uses our flesh a lot. Everybody is vulnerable. Look, the devil is like a thief who wears different kinds of cloths for operation against mankind...

SCENE FIVE B

(The scene returns to Ajoke and Lanre talking.)
LANRE: Promise me you'll not be offended if I tell you what's in my mind.
AJOKE: Tell me anything. I'll not take offence.
LANRE: Thank you. I have a feeling that if you're born-again, you'll not take your friend to the house where she killed her husband, the landlord. If you have preached to her, her husband would still be alive by now.
AJOKE: *(looks furious.)* What do you mean by that?
LANRE: You promised me you'll not be offended.
AJOKE: You're accusing me of aiding Lydia to kill her husband?
LANRE: I didn't say that!
AJOKE: Your mother, the prostitute, husband snatcher is the cause of his death.
LANRE: You need to give your life to Christ, ma, if you don't want the

devil to use you again and if you don't want to end up in hell. *(He quickly goes to join the rest, making her to boil with burning anger.)*
AJOKE: May God strike you dead!
LANRE: *(practically runs away from her.)* That will go back to sender in Jesus' name!

SCENE SIX

(Ibunkun is in the house eating gari as Ajoke walks briskly from the street to Ibunkun's house and knocks at the door.)
IBUNKUN: *(inside the room.)* Who is it?
AJOKE: It's your friend, Ajoke
IBUNKUN: You can come inside. *(Ajoke comes inside the room.)* You're welcome.
AJOKE: *(looks cheerful.)* Good afternoon, my friend.
IBUNKUN: *(gestures to the chair.)* You can have your seat. *(Ajoke sits close her.)* How are you and the children?
AJOKE: We're doing fine. Thank you.
IBUNKUN: You don't mind sharing this meal with me. I know it's not your stuff.
AJOKE: *(laughs.)* When you know it's not my stuff, why asking me to join me? *(She looks round.)* Where are the children?
IBUNKUN: They've all gone to the Church.
AJOKE: I came for two things. One of them is to report your son, Lanre, to you.
IBUNKUN: *(frowns.)* What did he do wrong?
AJOKE: He said I'm responsible for the death of Lydia's husband. *(Ibunkun frowns.)* I suppose he didn't tell you he said that to me last week? He even cursed me...
IBUNKUN: What? *(She shakes her head thoughtfully.)* Are you sure he said that?
AJOKE: You don't believe me, do you?
IBUNKUN: It's hard to believe... I mean he's not that kind of person...
AJOKE: Well, I suppose he's upset... He's just a teenager. So I've forgiven him. I would not have brought it up if I know he didn't tell you. Let's forget it.
IBUNKUN: I'm sorry for whatever he might have said to you.
AJOKE: It's okay.
IBUNKUN: What's the second thing you want to tell me?
AJOKE: I just come to tell you that I've found a native doctor that will help you with your financial condition.

IBUNKUN: *(looks a little confused and thoughtful.)* But I didn't say you should help me find a native doctor, did I?
AJOKE: I pity your condition, especially when I heard what made you start an affair with your late landlord. *(She gestures at the gari.)* See what you are eating when your mates are taking better meal. Even their dogs will not eat this type of food.
IBUNKUN: *(shrugs.)* I believe the food is one thing. The appetite to eat it is quite another thing though both are blessings.
AJOKE: You need to get rid of that mentality and understand that you're suffering. If you don't know that, consider the condition of your children, especially the little ones.
IBUNKUN: *(looks thoughtful.)* What do you suggest I should do now?
AJOKE: Let's go and see the native doctor first. He'll tell us what to do. *(Ibunkun looks reluctant.)* Come on....
IBUNKUN: Well, if what he says does not go down well with me, you'll have to count me out.
AJOKE: *(shrugs.)* Okay...

SCENE SEVEN A
(Awojebe is in the shrine when Awoseun appears.)
AWOSEUN: You did it, father! The woman is coming with her friend.
AWOJEBE: It is the gods that did it, not me. The woman you call her friend is not really her friend. She is just a messenger of the gods. You can give me the chain before they come, so that they can see you. *(Awoseun removes the chain on his neck and gives it to him. A while later, they hear Ajoke's voice outside.)*
AJOKE: Good afternoon, Baba....
AWOJEBE: Is that you, my daughter, Ajoke.
AJOKE: Yes, baba. I come with my friend.
AWOJEBE: Please, come inside. *(Ajoke with Ibunkun who looks round with a slightly confused expression enters.)* You're welcome. Please sit down.
AJOKE: Thank you, baba. *(She gestures at Ibunkun as they sit on the mat that is laid on the floor.)* This is my friend I told you about. *(Ibunkun bows her head in polite greetings.)*
AWOJEBE: You're welcome. *(He gestures at Awoseun who stands beside him.)* This is my son, Awoseun.
AJOKE: Good afternoon.
AWOSEUN: *(bows.)* You're welcome, ma.
AWOJEBE: *(looks at Awoseun.)* Please, excuse us. *(Awoseun*

leaves the place.)

AJOKE: As I told you, this friend of mine is having some problems which I know you can handle.

AWOJEBE: *(nods slowly with understanding.)* I see... *(He looks at Ibunkun.)* You have a very good friend who takes your problem as hers.

IBUNKUN: *(looks at Ajoke and smiles.)* Thank you.

AWOJEBE: Well, I need to consult the oracles about your case. That's the way I can get solution to the problem. Give me a minute. *(He stands up to leave the place.)*

SCENE EIGHT

(Awojebe enters strong house that is full of many fetish items, making incantations. After a awhile, a demon appears, roaring with laughter.)

AWOJEBE: *(goes on his kneels.)* You are welcome, my lord. The woman have come to us as we planned. What do I demand from her before we get her problem solved.

DEMON: Well done, my dedicated servant. I want you to tell the woman that if she wants all her problems to be solved and if she wants to live in luxuries, she needs to sacrifice the future of her favourite child to me.

AWOJEBE: What does that mean, my lord?

DEMON: You will make her understand that the money this child is to make in future is what will come to her but it goes beyond that. The truth is: the child will not live long before he dies once she gives you his name. You'll come here and conjures the spirit of the child. *(The demon disappears at once and Awojebe stands up to go.)*

SCENE SEVEN B

(Ibunkun and Ajoke are still sitting at the shrine when Awojebe enters.)

AJOKE: You're welcome, baba.

AWOJEBE: *(sits down, heaving a sigh of relief.)* Thank you, my daughter. *(He looks at Ibunkun.)* I've talked with the oracle. Your case is a very simple one with simple solution.

AJOKE: What makes it simple, baba?

AWOJEBE: Well, all she needs to give me is the name of her favourite child.

IBUNKUN: *(looks confused.)* Baba, can we leave my children out of this? I mean I'm doing all these because of them.

AWOJEBE: You don't even allow me to die before you begin to dig my grave. Let me explain the implication. *(He signs.)* The oracle told me that the child you love most will become wealthy in the next thirty or forty years.

IBUNKUN: *(looks surprised.)* Aaah!

AWOJEBE: If you can wait till then, you don't need me. If you can't wait, then you'll need to get the money the child is going to make in future. Believe me, that is a lot of money.

AJOKE: Is the child going to die.

AWOJEBE: Of course not! If he or she is going to die, I wont say it's a simple one.

AJOKE: It's simple indeed. Can it be applicable to me too?

AWOJEBE: I don't think so. It's unusual to have an easy one like this.

AJOKE: *(looks at Ibunkun).* This is a piece of cake for you. You better grab it while you have the chance! *(Ibunkun looks thoughtful for a while.)* What's the matter now?

IBUNKUN: I'm thinking about it.

AJOKE: Look, my friend, you better grab it. You may not see another easy way out of your financial problem.

IBUNKUN: Okay. Okay I'll do it.

AWOJEBE: If you're going to do it, we have to do it right away. What's the name of your favourite child?

IBUNKUN: He's Lanre. He's the oldest of my children.

AWOJEBE: Well, let's begin the work right away. *(He looks round.)* I need my son to assist me in the work. *(He calls out.)* Awoseun! *(There is voice outside that replies.)* I think he's at the backyard. *(He stands up.)* Let's go to the place we'll do the work. *(The women stand up.)*

EPISODE THREE

THE UNSEEN TORMENTOR

SCENE ONE

(Lanre comes into the room with a small bag. The children are eating some biscuits with water.)

1ST CHILD: You brought us some food! *(The children quickly open the bag.)* Rice! Beans!

2ND CHILD: And spaghetti! *(He looks at him.)* Where do you get it?

LANRE: Jesus gave it to us.

1ST CHILD: *(frowns at him.)* How?

2ND CHILD: He drops it from the sky, isn't it?

LANRE: No. God is not a magician to do that. He's a miracle working God. So he told someone in the Church to give the food to us. *(He smiles to him, leading them in the song, he begins to sing.)*

> He's a miracle working God
> Hallelujah
> He's a miracle working God
> He's the Alpha and Omega
> He's a miracle working God
>
> Singing hallelujah
> Amen, Amen!
> Hallelujah...

(As they sing, he drums the table.)

SCENE TWO A

(Awojebe is in the strong room with Awoseun, Ajoke and Ibunkun. Awojebe makes some incantations, performing some rituals like sprinkling some blood on an idol, holding a dead cock in his left hand.)

AWOJEBE: *(pauses in front of the idol.)* The oracle has spoken about what should be done about the case of Ibunkun Ilaran. *(He looks at Ibunkun.)* You can kneel before the god of the world. *(She looks reluctant.)* Are you changing your mind at this stage? *(She looks thoughtful.)* This is no time to think again because you cannot back out the moment you entered this place. *(He points at the front of the idol.)* Now, go and kneel over there. *(She slowly* *goes to kneel down.)* Ibunkun Ilaran has accepted to the offer you her son by giving you the name of her favourite child as you requested. The name of the child is Lanre Ilaran. Lanre has a bright future. So her mother agrees to be getting the money he is supposed to be making in future. I will call his name to you three times. As soon as I called the name the third time, let the deeds be done... Lanre Ilaran ooo... *(He begins to make incantations.)*

SCENE ONE B

(Lanre is till with other children, chatting.)
LANRE: When God gives me the job I'm praying for, I'll take good care of you and mummy.
1ST CHILD: We'll eat anything we like?
LANRE: Oh, sure! You'll continue your school.
2ND CHILD: *(looks excited.)* Really?
LANRE: Yes... *(He frowns all of a sudden.)*
1ST CHILD: What's wrong?
LANRE: Jesus is telling me to pray now.
1ST CHILD: Jesus? How does he speak to you? I can't hear him.
LANRE: I can hear him. *(He stands up.)* You can go and play outside. I have to pray now. *(The children leave the room. Lanre closes the door. After they leave, he begins to sing and pray.)*

> I'm serving a God of miracle!
> I know, yes, I know...
>
> I have a God who never fail...
> Who never fail...
> Who never fail forever more
> Amen! Jesus never fail!

(He begins to pray fervently.)

SCENE TWO B

AWOJEBE: *(makes incantations for a awhile.)* This is the third time I am going to call your name. When I call, let the deeds be done! Lanre oooo! *(A demon appears with great roar. The two women shrink backward with fear.)*
DEMON: I am not Lanre as you request. I am the spirit that is going to perform the deeds.
AWOJEBE: If that be the case, go and perform the deeds.

DEMON: Don't forget that the deed is to kill Lanre.
IBUNKUN: *(looks horrified.)* No! That's not the deed!
DEMON: I'm going after Lanre's life before I give you the money.
IBUNKUN: I don't want the money again if you're going to kill my son!
   (Ibunkun runs out of the place frantically. Ajoke attempts to go after her but Awojebe raise up his hand.)
AWOJEBE: If you follow her, you're a dead woman.
AJOKE: *(looks stunned but she stops.)* Aah!

SCENE ONE C
(Lanre is still praying and singing.)

LANRE: The God that answers by fire
   Let Him be my God...

   Unquestionable, you're the Lord...

   Eternal Rock of Ages
   I worship you, I adore
   Eternal Rock of Ages...
   You're the Lord...

(As he is praying and singing, the demon appears. There is a thunder that strikes, making the demon to disappear. Lanre continues to sing.)

   I give glory to the Lord
   He reigns...
   He reigns, He reigns
   I give glory to the Lord
   He reigns...
   Adoration
   Adoration to the Lord
   He reigns...

SCENE THREE
(Ibunkun runs towards the Church and begins to pray fervently as she walks for a while.)

SCENE TWO C
(Awojebe is making incantations with Ajoke and Awoseun

watching him. After a while, the demon appears again, looking furious.)
AWOJEBE: Have you performed the assignment?
DEMON: No!
AWOJEBE: *(looks surprised.)* Why not?
DEMON: The young man is untouchable! How dare you sent me to someone like that?
AWOJEBE: I... I didn't know there are some people you cannot touch.
DEMON: By now, you ought to know the limit of the power of Lucifer. *(Ajoke looks frightened.)* For not knowing, I'm going to suck the blood of each of you! *(He points at him, Awoseun and Ajoke.)*
AWOJEBE: That is a taboo! No one can use the children of a grand demon to appease a lesser demon. No chicken ever eat their own kind, no matter how they are hungry!
DEMON: You think so! *(He points at him. A ray of blue light flashes from him and reaches Awojebe, making him to fall down, emitting smoke and blood through his mouth, shaking violently until he dies. The other two are horror stricken. After a brief moment, the two of them run out of the place, going to different directions.)*

SCENE THREE

(The pastor is in the Church with Ibunkun, talking.)
IBUNKUN: *(tearfully looks at him.)* ...This is what happened, Pastor. *(She kneels before Pastor who looks thoughtful for a while.)* Please, ask God to forgive me and save me and my children. I've learnt my lesson. I'll serve Jesus for the rest of my life if he delivers me and my children. *(She covers her face and begins to sob hysterically).*
PASTOR: *(stands up thoughtfully and pulls her to the seat.)* I can assure you of one thing. No one can touch Lanre, your son because he's a child of God and the Bible says in Psalm 105 verse 14 and 15 that God permits no one do him wrong. He rebuked kings for his sake, saying, "touch not my anointed and do my prophets no harm." *(He sits down again, looking at her.)* But my concern is you. After all I told you about walking with Christ and after all the Church has done to help you meet your needs at home, you still went to patronize your enemies and the enemies of God.
IBUNKUN: *(sobs hysterically.)* I'm... so... sorry.
PASTOR: This will probably teach you a valuable lesson that you don't get free lunch from anyone except God. If the devil gives you a

thing, you can be sure he is going to take a much more valuable thing from you. Assuming he succeeds in taking your son from you, do you think he will stop there? No! A lot of people like you don't know that if you eat the food of the enemy of mankind, you'll pay for it with the priceless gift of God which is salvation though Jesus Christ. Materialism, pride of life, lust of the flesh are tools which the devil uses mostly to steal people from God, kill then spiritually and destroy them eternally in hell fire. No one can afford to take anything from the devil, not even from this world. After all, if you make all th money in the world, you're not going to take anything with you when you die. I know that it is not easy to be a Christian in this materialistic world. In fact Jesus said in Matthew chapter 7 verse 13 and 14 that the way to eternal life is narrow and very difficult it to follow. That's why very few people are taking the way. The way to hell, according to the passage is very broad. It is very convenient and in fact enjoyable to follow. You have to shun the easy way out of your problem. We all need the grace of God before we can follow the narrow way to heaven. *(He pauses to study her face.)* I want you to go to the alter over there... *(He points at the place.)* Confess all your sins to God and ask Him to forgive you. I'll pray with you before we go. *(Ibunkun nods vigorously and goes to the alter to lie down on her face, praying tearfully.)*

SCENE FOUR

(Ajoke runs frantically in the bush, panting heavily. She looks round nervously and begins to walk, looking very tired. The demon appears in front of her. She screams on top of her voice.)
DEMON: You can't run from me, woman.
AJOKE: *(goes on her kneels, still panting.)* Please, don't kill me.
DEMON: If I don't kill you, you'll go round the town, telling people what happened. If you do that, people will not consider Satan as a god and the king of the world again.
AJOKE: I promise I wont tell anyone.
DEMON: To help you keep that promise, you can go mad right now! *(Then he disappears. Ajoke begins to act as if she has gone crazy.)*

SCENE FIVE

(Lanre is reading the Bible in the room. After a while, the door opens and Ibunkun leads Pastor inside. Lanre stands up to greet then as they enter the room. Ibunkun who looks very remorseful

stands by the door while Pastor smilingly goes to the chair beside Lanre.)
LANRE: You're welcome, sir.
PASTOR: Thank you. *(He sits down beside him.)*
LANRE: *(looks at Ibunkun.)* Where have you been, mum? Church?
PASTOR: Yes, she came to the Church from somewhere.
LANRE: *(looks at him.)* Where, sir? *(There is a brief silence. He looks at Ibunkun for an answer.)* Why do you look so worried, mum?
PASTOR: Lanre, sit down. *(Lanre looks at him briefly before he sits down. Pastor looks at Ibunkun and gestures her to sit as well. Ibunkun silently sits beside Lanre.)* Well, Lanre, God has performed another major miracle.
LANRE: You got me the job?
PASTOR: Oh, no. Not yet. Getting you a job is not a major miracle - not even close to it.
LANRE: Well, I can't make a guess right now. I'm actually eager to hear it.
PASTOR: Your mother just become truly born-again.
LANRE: *(looks at Ibunkun briefly before he looks at Pastor again.)* Was she not born-again before now.
PASTOR: Actually no. She allowed herself to be influenced by her enemy that posed as a friend to take some unholy steps.
LANRE: *(looks disappointed.)* Well, sir, I was hoping you would tell me some good news and...
PASTOR: Hey, Lanre. You have the greatest miracle and the most precious gift from God, which you must appreciate first. People often don't know the value of life until they realize the until they've gone through battle of life. *(He pats him on the shoulder.)* You've gone through battle but you don't seem to know it.
LANRE: We've always gone though battle since I was born - battle with poverty, sickness, sorrow, pains and a host of others.
PASTOR: *(smiles.)* Those are general battles of life. The battle I'm talking about is the one Jesus is fighting for you right now - the battle which your mother witnessed. *(Lanre frowns at him. Pastor looks at Ibunkun.)* You can tell him what happened.
IBUNKUN: *(in a gentle voice.)* Lanre, would you forgive me if I tell you?
LANRE: Of course, I will, no matter what it is.
IBUNKUN: Thank you. *(She looks thoughtful for a while before she begins.)* I felt what we were going through was unbearable. So

I tried to find an easy way out of our multiple financial problems. This made me get involved with what caused the Landlord's death. I took the advice of someone I thought was my friend and went to a witch doctor ....

SCENE SIX

(Awoseun is screaming and running in the bush. He frantically bursts into Ogunjola's consulting room, painting heavily.)

OGUNJOLA: *(looks startled.)* Why do you burst in like that, son of Awojebe?

AWOSEUN: *(breathlessly.)* My father...

OGUNJOLA: What's wrong with him?

AWOSEUN: He's dead!

OGUNJOLA: *(springs up.)* Impossible! What could have possibly caused the death of a strong man like that?

AWOSEUN: *(pants.)* It's a long story, baba - a very long story.

OGUNJOLA: Let's go and confirm if he's really dead.

AWOSEUN: He's dead! I saw how the whole thing happened.

OGUNJOLA: Let's go there still. There may be something I can do to bring him back.

AWOSEUN: I'm not going back there.

OGUNJOLA: *(looks puzzled.)* What not?

AWOSEUN: The spirit that killed him is trying to take my life as well.

OGUNJOLA: And you think you can escape from him by running?

AWOSEUN: At least, I can run to the person that defeated the spirit...

OGUNJOLA: *(looks thoughtful for a while.)* I'll go and see your father first before I know what to do. *(The two of them leave the room.)*

SCENE SEVEN

(Ajoke acts like a mad woman in the street with people looking at her with wonder. She goes from place to place, picking things up and laughing. She sees someone selling some bread. She goes to grab a loaf. When the seller attempts to take it from her, she begins to run. She runs after her.)

SCENE EIGHT

(Ogunjola enters the room where Awojebe's dead body is still lying. He looks agitated as he examines the body. He soon begins to recite some incantations. After a while he looks downward hopelessly, shaking his head with despair.)

OGUNJOLA: The gods must have struck down the giant elephant! Who is going to bring him up again? *(He shakes his head in hopeless gestures.)*

SCENE NINE

(Awoseun runs frantically towards Lanre's house. Pastor is still with Ibunkun and Lanre in the room when Awoseun bursts in, panting heavily. The rest looks startled.)

IBUNKUN: *(in a surprised tone.)* What do you want here?

AWOSEUN: *(pants.)* I'm sorry to burst in like that. *(He looks at Lanre.)* Lanre, I need your help. *(The other two men look surprised.)*

LANRE: How do you know my name?

IBUNKUN: He's the son of the witch doctor that wanted to help me make quick money.

PASTOR: I see... *(He looks at Awoseun.)* What help do you need from him?

AWOSEUN: Shortly after she left... *(He points at Ibunkun.)* The spirit that was sent to suck his blood ... *(He points at Lanre.)* ... returned and killed my father. *(The rest look more surprised.)* He turned the woman that brought her into a mad woman. The spirit is now running after me. *(He falls on his kneels before Lanre.)* He plans to kill me. Please, help me! I'll do anything you want me to do. *(There is brief thoughtful silence.)*

LANRE: What makes you think I can help you?

AWOSEUN: I know you serve a big God. The spirit confirms it.

LANRE: Well, I can't handle this case. *(He gestures at Pastor.)* Meet my Pastor. He can handle it.

AWOSEUN: *(looks hopefully at Pastor.)* Please, help me, Pastor; I'll do anything to be free from the spirit of death.

PASTOR: *(signs.)* Sit down. *(Awoseun sits down slowly.)* Jesus is the only one that can deliver you if we pray to Him. Before we pray for the spirit to leave you alone, you must hear the word of God first. *(Awoseun nods vigorously.)* You'll do what I tell you? *(Awoseun again nods as Pastor takes the Bible with him and opens it.)* I want to share with you the weight of death. A lot of people don't know the weight of death because they don't know anything about eternal life and eternal death. In the gospel according to Saint John chapter 3 verse 16, the Bible says, "for God so loved the world, especially you and everybody, including me that He gave his only begotten Son that whoever, including witch doctors, cult members, sinners and wicked people, believes in Jesus should not perish but have everlasting life. The word "perish" means eternal death in hell fire. Eternal life means the life in heaven. Only Jesus can make someone like you and me worthy to have eternal life. So Jesus Christ came into the world to die for our sins. All we need to do is to give our lives to Him before we can become children of God, according to John chapter 1 verse 12. The weight of death is found in the lake that burns with fire and brimstone. Anybody serving the devil either directly as in your case or indirectly through sins and lust of the flesh will feel the weight of death when he dies and goes right straight to hell. What is pursuing you right now is a child's play when you compare it to what will happen to you if you die in your sin. So for you to be free from this spirit and have eternal life, you need to give your life to Jesus Christ right now. Are you ready to do that?

AWOSEUN: *(quickly.)* Yes, Pastor, I'm ready.

PASTOR: You'll surrender your life to Jesus right now and burn all the charms and other things that'll take you to hell. Are you ready to do that?

AWOSEUN: Yes, I'm ready.

PASTOR: You can kneel down and let's pray. *(Awoseun kneels down.)* Close your eyes and begin to confess all your sins. **(As Awoseun obeys.)**

SCENE TEN

(Ajoke runs round the street until she runs into a car that knocks her down. She dies on the spot with blood spilling through her mouth.)

SCENE ELEVEN

(Awoseun stands by as he burns all the fetish items. After a while, the demon appears, roaring with laughter. Awoseun looks puzzled.)

DEMON: What do you think you're doing, son of Awojebe?

AWOSEUN: I'm burning all the items that link me to you and your master, Satan.

DEMON: You're such a fool... Do you think it's easy to get rid of me like that?

AWOSEUN: Why not? It's not by my power or might but by the Spirit of the Lord.

DEMON: I'm your god, remember? Your father served me till he dies. So you must serve me too!

AWOSEUN: Why should I serve you? My father served you but you killed and took him to hell. I have a new Master. He is my God now. He is the King of kings and Lord of lords.

DEMON: Shut up there! I am your god. If you don't serve me, you'll die!

AWOSEUN: You're not my God. My God has a name above every other names. His word says that at the sound of His name, every knee must bow and every tongue must confess that JESUS IS LORD! *(There is a great thunder. The demon disappears at once. Awoseun begins to sing.)*

> I have a God who never fails…
> Amen Jesus never fails
> Jesus never fails forever more....

CHECK OUT OTHER BOOKS BY DIPO TOBY ALAKIJA
Each Serves Either As Edifying Or Evangelical Or Missionary Or Academic Tool At Home, School, Bible Clubs, Sunday Schools, Church, Office And Other Fellowships

FOOTSTEPS IN THE MUD
ISBN: 978-36348-9-5 ISBN: 978-978-36348-9-3

The Drama Package Of Results Of Research Works That trace Global And Societal Vices To The Corrupt Or Lost Of Family Values

The 13-Episode drama book involves Bosede who learnt many wrong things from her parents' conduct and foul language. She was forced to marry Kola when she became pregnant. Using her mother's method to handle her father, she tried to subject Kola to her control. In the course of that, she made life terrible for him. Although her mother tried to warn her of the implications of maltreating her husband but Bosede has grown out of control. Consequently, while looking for peace, Kola was pushed out of the house. He made friends with some guys who taught him the unholy ways of life and influenced him to become a menace in the house.

Junior who was born at time the couple never proved to be responsible parents also learnt wrong things from them. He decided to follow his father's footsteps by taking alcohol when he was in primary school. As if that was not bad enough, he tried to teach other children in the school the madness in his home. A school teacher, however, was able to influence him and his mother by teaching them Christian morals. Even then, Junior was soon caught in the crossfire at home as his father tried to enlist him as a future member of a secret cult that posed as a social club.

RANSOM FOR LOVE
ISBN: 978-49874-8-1 ISBN: 978-978-4987-4-8-6

She accepted his marriage proposal without knowing the kind of person he was. She soon discovered that he was a mean and ruthless guy who was always ready to get whatever he wanted by all means even if he has to pay for it with the lives of others. She was in his bondage, especially when her parents who believed he was a generous and gentleman were on his side.

Because she considered the proposal to marry him as a marriage engagement with the devil incarnate, she decided that she would rather die than to share her life with him. Then out of the blues, this passionate gentleman sneaked into her life despite all she did to discourage him. She could not resist his love for her when he offered to set her free from the devil incarnate. Then the battle began – sooner than they anticipated.

NO MORE TEARS TO SHED
ISBN: 978-49874-3-0 ISBN: 978-978-74-3-1

Kidnappers took Tokunbo away from his grand parents in a city in Nigeria when he was a little boy. A nice woman found him in another town and gave him a false identity. She spoilt him with love, making him to grow into a rebellious teenager that was not appreciated anywhere. When Janet made him a Christian, however, life began to make sense to him until the day he was beaten to the point of death for the offence he knew nothing about. He left the town for the city which, unknown to him, held his true identity and the link to his parents in the United States. To find them was only a question of time.

THE UNROMANTIC LOVE BIRDS
ISBN: 978-4987-5-7 ISBN: 978-978-4974-5-5
And other short stories about love and marriages

They were very much in love right from their school days but when they got married and had children, romance became the game Charles' wife refused to play. No matter how much he tried to make her understand the unbearable condition her unromantic attitude has subjected him into, she would not change. Consequently, after enduring for so long, he was forced to look for the women that would make up for her weakness. He unofficially married a beautiful lady of insane jealousy. Though she was ready to give him what was missing in his marriage, it soon dawn on him that he has solved one big problem only to create a bigger one.

THE BATTLE OF THE CONQUERORS
ISBN: 978-49874-7-3 ISBN: ISBN: 978-978-49874-0-7-9

Wickedness takes over the land of Bondage from First Couple and subjects everybody into slavery without giving anybody the chance to be free. Love brings The Redeemer from Eternity and offers the slaves the chance to escape. Wickedness soon declares war and engages everyone in the battle. The Redeemer makes the redeemed people Conquerors by giving them the armour of war and Comforter but

Wickedness cannot be undone. He has several thousands of years of experience in the war. So he is quick to recognize the weakness of the redeemed people who are ignorant of their strengths and advantages. Although the Conquerors fight like immutable giants, rescuing victims of war, many people suffer heavy casualties.

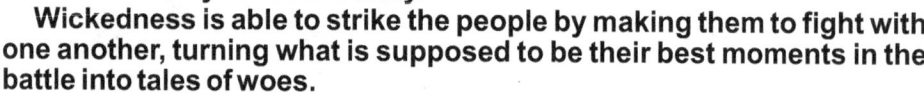

Since King Wickedness knows that a redeemed person is strong enough to chase one thousand of his warriors at a time, and two would put ten thousand into flight, he enlists as one of his warriors the people's deadliest enemy called Disunity.

Wickedness is able to strike the people by making them to fight with one another, turning what is supposed to be their best moments in the battle into tales of woes.

BLOODSHED IN CAMPUS
ISBN: 978-07350-3-8 ISBN: 978-978-07350-3-6

A poor widow tearfully warned her son, Richard, against joining the bad wagon when he got an admission into one of the Nigerian Universities. He resisted the membership of groups of students, including the Christian Fellowship until he had an encounter with a member of The Black Skulls - a deadly and ruthless secret cult on the campus.

Before Richard knew what he was up against, the head of The Black Skulls had arranged items for his initiation into the cult. While resisting being initiated, he ran to the Christian Fellowship for help. The leader of the Christian Fellowship dragged The President of Students' Union Government (S.U.G) into the conflict. With the involvement of the S.U.G President, another formidable cult called The Red Eyes felt obliged to team up against The Black Skulls. Then the campus turned into a battlefield and BLOODSHED became the order of the black day.

NETWORK BIBLE CLUB
YOUTH AND ADULT BOOK ONE
ISBN: 978 - 978- 49874-9-X ISBN: 978-978-49874-9-3

A collection of 26 life transforming stories, 26 poems, 26 hymn tuned songs and weekly Bible lessons

The issue of moral instructions in schools and at homes is threatened with extinction. Consequently, so many youths are involved in prostitution, drug addictions, cultism, fraudulent practices, armed robberies and other crimes. Those who are supposed to be trained as leaders in various walks of life are the ones posing serious threats to many lives. Many parents who fail to add moral values to the upbringing of their children often times breed potential criminals under their roofs without knowing it. Apart from these, many other people negatively influence young ones through the media, music, publications, films, conduct and foul language; making them to lose their moral and family values.

This book one just like the rest of other volumes is an attempt to bring back moral instructions into schools and campuses through the use of stories, hymn tuned songs, poems, Bible lessons and class activities. It is designed to assist teachers and ministers in Secondary Schools, Bible Clubs, Churches and Campus Fellowships to teach people, especially youths the Word of God and serves as a school text book in subjects relating to literature, music and other creative works.

FOUNDATION BIBLE CLUB A-Z STORY BOOK
ISBN: 978-49874-2-2 ISBN: 978-978-49874-2-4
Volume 1 With 26 Stories, 26 Bible Lessons, 26 Rhymes And 26 Songs For Book For Young Minds

An adage says, "a man who builds a house without building his child builds what the child will later sell." Proverbs 22:6 says, "train up a child in the way he should go: and when he is old, he will not depart from it." This book is an attempt to assist parents and teachers to meet up to the challenges that befall them in carrying out this important function in the light of the moral decadence that is prevailing all over the world.

The first edition of the book was used by several thousands of teachers, ministers and parents in schools, Churches and homes to build the moral values of young ones. Apart from the stories, songs and Bible passages for the young ones to study, there is a seminar material that is based on the lecture which the author delivered to school proprietors, children ministers and Christian professionals in this volume.

SUCCESSFUL CHRISTIANITY AND BASIC MINISTRIES
ISBN: 978-49874-6-0
A Collection Of Resource Materials That Precedes Christian Ministries And Basic Leadership Course Book

The first question is how Christianity is practiced even in a hostile environment. Next to that is the question about the potentials of Christians in spite of their apparent limitations. The other issues are connected to the successes, deliverance, callings, basic ministries of all Christians and evangelism. Various schools of thoughts have attempted these questions but many answers only portray Christianity as a form of religion instead of a way of life as specified by God. Some answers give room for compromise, hypocrisies, dogmas and denominational doctrines. The misconceptions about these areas of Christianity have brought about worldliness instead of righteousness and false achievements instead of fulfillment.

This book which contains six different subjects had been used to hold seminars at various levels, train ministers and Christian workers in Bible Schools and to equip the Church. It explains in simple terms the seemingly complex issues on practice of Christianity, Potentials, Deliverance, God's Kind Of Success, Evangelism and Basic Ministries of a Christian with Biblical principles, life transforming stories and illustrations.

CHRISTIAN MINISTRIES AND BASIC LEADERSHIP
ISBN: 978-36348-7-9 ISBN: 978-978-36348-7-9
A Collection Of Resource Materials That Follows Up Successful Christianity And Basic Ministries Course Book

As it is common to say that the hood does not make a monk, the dignified positions and bogus titles of many Christian leaders in modern days do not really make them Gospel Ministers.

This course book - a compilation of five resource materials on Missions And Outreach Ministries, Christian Communication Arts, Christian Leadership, Christian Education Methodology and Ministries Of Improvisations - aims at making every matured Christian an effective minister and leader at their respective homes, communities and nations. It teaches various ways Christians can communicate the word of God, meeting up to their responsibilities as ministers and leaders that reconcile people to God, edifying the Body Of Christ and reaching out to souls at the same time.

All of the resource materials are in use in Bible Schools like College Of Christian Education And Missions, in Churches and other ministries to raise Christian workers, Evangelists, Missionaries and other Ministers that serve at various levels and leadership capacities.

INSANITY OF HUMANITY
ISBN: 978-36348-6-0 ISBN: 978-978-36348-6-2
The Results Of Research Works Into Various Methods Of Brainwashing

Man is made to exercise his freewill. The mind of his own and the power to choose between right and wrong, good and evil, light and darkness is about to be washed away through brainwashing. The agents of control dubbed as Secret Government by John Todd (the top

Illuninati defector) have put necessary machinery in place to ensure that all human beings are in conformity in their thinking and ways of life, trying to wipe away diversity, which makes each person unique.

This book attempts to shed light on how the techniques of mind control are applied through the use of propaganda, education, entertainments, drugs, religions, media and other means of communications. It is the result of research works, some of which are based on findings of various researchers and writers like Bugger Lugz, Edward Hunter, Hadley Cantril, Herbert Krugman, David L. Robb, Vaughan Bell, Juliana Gomez, Ryan Duffy Vice, Henry Makow, David Nicholls, Fritz Springmeire, Steven Hassan, Renate Thienel, Debra Pursell, Mary Pride and a host of others who are acknowledged in this book.

CALVARY ROCK RESOURCE BOOKLETS

The Quarterly Missionary Booklets That Are Designed To Teach Children, Youths And Adults In Schools, Fellowships, Churches, At Homes, Office And Other Places.

Although all the various volumes of this booklet can be used independently of other books but it is recommended that it should be used as part of supplementary materials to make up for Foundation and Network Bible Club Story Books for both children and adults in School, Church, Campus, Office and other Fellowships.

Each of the volume is rich with quarterly Bible lessons, stories, drama, songs, seminar, tract materials and a host of other things that can be used to edify, educate, entertains and evangelize every category of people, ranging from children to elderly persons.

Every volume is designed to equip school teachers, ministers in Churches or campus or office fellowships and other people who wish to work with the Lord.

All These And Other Books Are Distributed Worldwide And Published By The Publishing House Of Calvary Rock Resources

*Ikenne-Remo, Nigeria
*Manchester, United Kingdom
*New York, United States

www.calvaryrock.org

www.ingramcontent.com/pod-product-compliance
Lightning Source LLC
Chambersburg PA
CBHW031655040426
42453CB00006B/315